FOOTBALL LEXICON

LEIGH is a Sheffield Wednesday ⬛⬛⬛
WOODHOUSE supports Aston ⬛⬛⬛

Further praise for *Football Lexicon*:

'Excellent … *Football Lexicon* deals only in the finest clichés, those that footballers, commentators and writers use in all seriousness, most of the time without even knowing it.' *Observer Sport Monthly*

'A catalogue of clichés, a sort of Robbie Fowler's *Modern English Usage* … A deliciously wry, witty gem.' *Time Out*

'Pleasingly self-mocking … This essential work sharply points out the inherent contradictions in much football speak.' *Times Literary Supplement*

'The best thing since *Roger's Profanisaurus* … It knits together the clichéd phrases we take for granted like a string of effortless Brazilian passes.' *Ice Magazine*

'Leigh & Woodhouse take an admirably detached view of football's language, rarely judging, just simply setting down the unbreakable laws of the commentator's jargon … This small, witty, neatly produced volume would be a nice loo book for any football fan, but there's one group of people who definitely shouldn't be without a copy. All aspiring football commentators must immediately learn the entire lexicon off by heart. Whatever the situation, they will never be lost for a cliché.' *Guardian*

'Excellent … You will be hard pressed to think of any of football's huge store of more or less viable tropes that they have missed … Leigh & Woodhouse are civilised guides to all that's tritest and best in football parlance.' *London Review of Books*

'A wickedly deadpan A-Z of argot … The lads show clinical finishing and give 200 per cent.' Boyd Tonkin, *Independent* (Books of the Year)

'Learned and informative, as well as entertaining.' *Programme Monthly and Football Collectable*

by the same authors
Racing Lexicon

FOOTBALL LEXICON

LEIGH & WOODHOUSE

faber and faber

In association with The Oleander Press

First published in 2004 by The Oleander Press
This paperback edition published in 2006
by Faber and Faber Limited
3 Queen Square London WC1N 3AU

Photoset by RefineCatch Ltd, Bungay, Suffolk
Printed in England by Mackays of Chatham Ltd

A CIP record for this book
is available from the British Library

ISBN 0-571-23052-0
ISBN 978-0-571-23052-5

2 4 6 8 10 9 7 5 3 1

Preface

Football fans don't only watch football. They talk it.
They listen to it. They need to read and hear all about
it. A whole industry, ranging from match commentaries and the sports pages of newspapers to radio
phone-ins and websites, caters for this need every day
of the week.

It has not always been thus. Originally, the task of
football commentators and reporters was that of con-
veying information for the benefit of those not present at a match. There was indeed once a fear that
people might be deterred from going to a match if
they knew it had been selected for live radio commentary. Hence the practice (which now looks quaint
and self-important) of not disclosing the location of
the honoured venue before kick-off. And even then
the commentator might reveal it in a tantalisingly
protracted way: 'To my right, I see lights coming on in
the flats and a wisp of smoke from a distant chimney,
while a flag flutters aloft on the stand opposite: yes, of
course, we're at the Dell for Southampton v Everton'.

This scruple was abandoned, not because it no
longer seemed that radio commentary could emulate
the actual experience of a match, but probably because

it was recognised that they could be complementary. Some fans indeed go to matches with headphones so they get both. But the shift indicates a more general sense that football commentary and reporting do more than meet the modest task of just providing information. They provide pleasures and fulfil needs which are more mysterious. Many fans rush from a game they have just seen to hear it reported on the radio, before buying a paper to read about it. Rarely is it information they want. Instead, it seems, they wish to see what the match which they have just experienced fleetingly, subjectively and intensely looks like in the words of someone else.

Television coverage of football, which, like radio commentary, was greeted with suspicion when it arrived, has also contributed to changing the nature of football reporting. It is now likely that many of those reading a report in a Sunday paper will have already seen on television, if not actually in the stadium, some of the action being described. Yet, if anything, this has liberated reporters from the more humble task of providing information to concentrate rather on description and discussion.

Moreover, now that players carry names on their shirts, cameramen can zoom in and out and we can activate buttons which provide statistics, you might have thought that television could dispense with commentators altogether, since we do not need them for information. Yet, in common with their counterparts working for newspapers, television commentators have found that their jobs have not been threatened but made more interesting by these changes. Running commentary has become so integral to our experience of football that you may hear children who are kicking a ball about in backstreets and schoolyards actually supply their own commentary as they dribble, shoot and foul, while computer games which simulate football matches, even as they indulge the fantasy that you are a Premiership footballer, sometimes provide a commentary in the language of your choice. For all the talk of a visual age, television coverage has made the experience of football even more verbal.

As coverage of football has spread from newspapers to radio and television, a morphology in the language with which it is described may be charted. All sports have their own jargon, their own linguistic idiosyncrasies. The language of football perhaps deserves especial attention. Firstly, of all sports, football seems to arouse in those who watch it the blindest loves and the bitterest hatreds. We watch our team with blinkers. Football commentators and reporters are by and large scrupulous in not allowing themselves to be infected in such a way, but most of them must suppress these emotions rather than just not have them. It follows that their language can be heavily euphemistic and also awkwardly hyperbolic on occasions. Secondly, the sheer quantity of matches covered, the pace at which football is played, and the remarkable speed with which journalists have to compile their reports, all necessitate a certain formulaic quality in responses to football. It is sometimes too easy to deplore as clichés the many phrases and words that can act as useful shorthand for the reader or listener. But while football matches are iterative and contain certain invariable situations, one match perhaps differs from another more than in any other sport. The language of commentators and reporters is restless and inventive too, as football matches and football itself take unpredictable turns.

But perhaps the most noticeable phenomenon has been the relatively recent discovery of the talking footballer or talking football manager. Interviews pre- and post-match have introduced us to a new vocabulary.

There was a time when footballers were working-class heroes who earned working-class wages. They might have lived down your street. Yet, unless they did so, they were to football supporters mute figures intermittently visible over a sea of clothcaps. Most people never heard them talk about a match, let alone read their opinions. Then footballers started to move in a different orbit from most of us. But, just as they have disappeared behind tinted windows and electronic gates, they have become more familiar to us than ever, through written and oral interviews. The contrast between the facility with which some stars express themselves on the pitch and their inarticulacy off it can be a source of embarrassment. Language to these footballers is like tarmac to their studs. But the contrast may also be a source of consolation. To an extent, laughter at the way they speak is the revenge of fans on the players they'd love to have been. The clichés and set phrases – sick as a parrot, over the moon, game of two halves – to which players and managers seem to turn at every juncture have indeed been echoed so gleefully and frequently by the public that the mockery of these commonplaces has itself become commonplace. Besides, the language of football players and managers has moved on. You will not hear these phrases at all these days, unless they come coated in irony. Other equally ossified terms may have taken their place, but in general a greater self-consciousness is to be found when players and managers speak. This may stem from the increased prominence of non-native speakers who, in some cases, are making English football discourse more improvised and eccentric, and, in other instances, are rendering it more deliberate and precise, the subset of a language that has actually been learned. At all events, clichés feature less commonly in their parlance. But the increased self-consciousness and variety of expression result more probably from the acknowledged fact that speaking to the press and handling the media are, if you will pardon the cliché, part and parcel of the modern game.

Footballers and their managers continue to be derided for clichés they no longer actually use. We do not intend to add to or update these catalogues, but to identify more pervasive usages, some admirably economic, others less felicitous, in an attempt to circumscribe the changing vocabulary of commentators and reporters as well as the discourse of footballers, to snapshot the contemporary mannerisms of the BBC and *The Times* as well as Robbie Fowler's modern English usage.

A

Academic: Of no import, of no consequence whatsoever. Likely to appeal chiefly, or only, to pedants: 'The Slovenia v Liechtenstein qualifier is of purely *academic* interest'. The adjective *academical* surfaces exclusively in the name of *Hamilton Academical*, a club whose small size and modest achievements emphasise, in tandem with the long name, the futile pretensions of anything *academic*. Yet the noun *Academy* is dignified. West Ham United *fancy themselves* in all seriousness as 'the *Academy* of Football'. Many other clubs like to name their youth development schemes in this way, however remote windswept training grounds may appear to be from the secluded groves of academia.

Account: Managers of lower-division clubs drawn against one of the ***big boys*** regularly limit their ambition to seeing their players give a *good account of themselves*. *By all accounts* is the standard phrase to indicate that the person speaking was not actually at the game he is talking about: '*By all accounts*, Tranmere were *full value* for their win last week at the Manor Ground'.

Acquaintance: Players who re-oppose *erstwhile* team-mates are said, often with a hint of irony, to *renew their acquaintance* with them. See also *warm welcome*. For more friendly circumstances, where a player *links up* with a former manager, the two parties tend to *renew their association* or *join up* once more. Although, on an off day, team-mates can play as if they have *only just met*.

Acquisition: Perhaps the most common synonym for *signing*. Clubs always *parade* or **unveil** their *recent acquisitions*, usually at a *hastily convened* press conference. Note though that some adjectives (like *astute* and *record*) more readily qualify *signing* rather than *acquisition*.

Acrobatic: An adjective often heard in commentary, even for actions which are not particularly *acrobatic*. Reserved especially for *overhead kicks* or *last-ditch clearances*. There can be a pejorative tinge when used of saves: 'Miklosko made that one look *acrobatic*'. See also *one for the **cameras***.

Adjudged: For some reason much more common than 'judged' when describing a refereeing decision: 'Grimandi was *adjudged* to have pulled Yorke back'. Takes the adverbs *rightly* or *harshly*.

Admission money: Unit of value for an **outrageous** piece of skill: 'That *drag back* from Zola was worth the *admission money* alone'. Uttered particularly by commentators who have not actually had to pay said *price of admission*.

Advantage: When a referee allows play to continue after a foul, to the *advantage* of the aggrieved team, fans and commentators alike are so amazed he did not blow his whistle when he could have done that the *advantage* is qualified as *good* or even *excellent*: 'The Spennymoor official having played an *excellent advantage*, Zico swung in a low cross and Eder made it 2-0'. The referee momentarily seems to become a player here, as once illustrated at Anfield when Mike Reed celebrated after an *advantage* he had *played* resulted in a goal. If the *advantage* does not *accrue* (a phrase more used in rugby) the ref is blamed for not *blowing up* rather than being criticised for a 'bad advantage', which would indeed sound strange.

Advert: Footballers have long since featured in commercials for male essentials – beer and shaving cream – but they can advertise the game itself: a thrilling match may be described as a *good advert for football*. This is more common than the now rather risible 'football was the winner today'. Sometimes, more specifically, a good game advertises the division, country or even continent in which it is being played: 'The match in Saitama, clinched by an Oguro goal in **stoppage** *time*, was a *fantastic advert* for the game in Asia'. If a national league has been criticised for its lack of entertainment value, a rousing contest can seem to have a more spiritual effect (even if advertising is still included for good measure): 'It was a match that did much to restore *faith* in the Barclays Premiership'.

Aerial: The idea of *aerial bombardment* or *aerial onslaught* compares teams of the Charles Hughes school of football to the squadrons of 'Bomber' Harris: 'Neil Warnock's **men** insisted on waging an *aerial war* which Calum Davenport won every time'. More commonly, the adjective is used to describe a particular *aerial tussle* or *aerial **battle*** between two players.

Affair: Generally a synonym for *match*, which can range from the jolly *all-ticket affair* (more worthy of note when you could just turn up and pay at the *gate*), through the *drab* or *lifeless affair*, to the *physical* or ***ill-tempered*** *affair*.

Afford: The verb invariably employed when somebody has *mythical* or *legendary* status at a club: 'Craig Madden is *afforded legendary* status at Gigg Lane'. A team can also *afford the **luxury*** of missing penalties or chances if they ultimately win.

Afters: Resumes the idea of *after* the tackle or challenge: 'There was a little bit of *afters* there between Mulryne and Magilton'. *Afters* can come before ***handbags***, perhaps counter-intuitively.

After you, Claude: Derives from the war-time radio show *It's That Man Again*, where one of the regular sketches featured two impossibly polite gentlemen whose exchange of catchphrases was '*After You, Claude*'; 'No, after you, Cecil'. Claude now seems to have barged Cecil out of the way, but the first part of the tag-line enjoys a strong afterlife in football. It can be used of fatal hesitation at one end of the pitch: 'Queen's Park nearly conceded a comic goal when Crawford and Agostini tried the old "*After you, Claude*" routine'. Or at the other: 'Some "*after you, Claude*" style attacking saw Butler, Plummer and Smeltz all take it in turns to pass when a shot seemed the better **option**'. It can also describe an ***academic*** end-of-season match: 'This was "*after you Claude*" *Makelele* fare: in the first half, especially, the game had the low-heat feel of a Community Shield'. In all cases, the social class assumed by the original Claude and Cecil may help to explain why the allusion is so favoured by old-school managers: 'If everyone stood back and said: "*After you, Claude*", it wouldn't be a spectacle. We mustn't have a football snobbery where people look down on *hard work*'.

Agony: Used in its original sense to describe the last moments before death, *agony* has been softened in general usage and diluted further by football, where it tends (in a strange meeting of the psychological and the physical) to be *piled on* by the opponents. A late sending off or the news of ***results** elsewhere* may even ***compound** the agony*. The adverb is regularly used of shots that just miss the target: 'Johanssen's *follow-up* trickled *agonisingly* wide'.

All about: 'That's what this ***football club*** is *all about*'. Managers, players and sometimes fans will use these summary words when swelling with pride about a spirited fightback, a tenacious ***rearguard*** action, a heroic collective effort in clearing the pitch of snow. But when, more commonly, you are shaking your head and commenting on an embarrassing defeat, it is customary to say something like: 'That's The Honest Men *for you*' or 'that's Manchester City *all over*'. See also ***way***.

All-action: Used adjectivally by *all-action* prose stylists of *live wires* and their *displays* or *performances*: 'Rookie Wayne Routledge was crowned king of the Palace as his *all-action display* grounded *nine-**man*** Bluebirds'.

All day: 'Yobo and Weir can ***deal with*** those kind of hopeful balls in *all day*'. The summariser is hardly expecting improbable amounts of *added time* here, but pointing out that Everton's defenders are not extended. In Sunday morning games, the goalkeeper and defenders may want to comment more sarcastically on an opponent's *woeful* finish: 'We'll *have* that *all day long*, pal'. Of course, the next attack will result in an *unstoppable* goal and an unprintable retort.

All of: Emphasises the full distance a ball or player has travelled, as if the commentator has physically paced out the distance: 'Jamie McAllister *thundered* an *unstoppable* left-footed shot past Gordon Marshall from *all of* 25 yards'; 'Edu ran *all of* thirty yards to get involved there, Martin'. Compare ***fully***.

Almighty: Some say football is an 'implicit religion'. A few words (***faithful***, ***fanatic***) support the idea. But *almighty* is used almost exclusively in football parlance to describe the very secular occurrence known as the *almighty scramble*.

Altercation: A rather euphemistic way of describing a *bust-up*, a *dust-up*, a ***situation*** where players square up, as in: 'Bit of an *altercation* off the ball there'. See also ***handbags***.

Always: Used, always in hindsight, to suggest an action was predestined: 'His header was *always* going wide'. An *emphatic* finish can be celebrated in similar fashion: 'That was going in *from the moment* the ball left Bobby Charlton's *boot*'.

Ambassador: Certain players have the qualities to merit being described as *great ambassadors* for the *club*, ***game***, or *sport*. Pelé, Franz Beckenbauer, Bobby Charlton and Bobby Moore are some of the usual suspects when it comes to receiving this epithet (or epitaph). Perhaps Pelé's credentials might need to be reviewed in the light of the following: 'He's been such a *great ambassador* for the *game* that it's sad to see Pelé doing adverts for the treatment of erectile dysfunction'.

Ambition: In football, *ambition* means 'money'. It is standard practice for a player to identify a *lack of ambition* as the reason for his leaving a club and equally conventional to praise his new paymasters as a *club with ambition*. No doubt it would sound heartless to turn your back on a club 'because it's got no money' and a little vulgar to sign for a club because 'they're paying me shedloads', but such sincerity would be refreshing. So often mocked for their ingenuous language, footballers learn their lines impeccably when it comes to the bottom line.

Ambitious: Pejorative when used in the course of a game, to describe overhit passes, abortive **one-twos** or improbable *long-range efforts*. But the adjective is positive when referring to managers, especially when they are young (and Scottish): 'He's a young, *ambitious* manager who wants to win things with this club'. It may sound as though there are other managers who do *not* want to win things, but an *ambitious* manager, and the *direction* the club is *going in*, constitute an integral part of the **set-up** lauded by new signings.

Anatomy: This word has long been serviceable for commentators who wish to avoid indiscretion: 'Someone in the wall's been hit in a *painful part* of the *anatomy*'. A feature too in post-match interviews with players who have **bundled** *in* a goal without necessarily *knowing much about it*: 'I'm not quite sure which part of my *anatomy* it's come off but it's in the **back of the net**'. It is when the stakes are highest that the crucial moment is liable to be a *scruffy* own goal or a **scuffed** penalty. The body parts involved become revered by the **faithful** as if they were the bones of saints, and the relics are duly commemorated in fanzine titles such as *Gary Mabbutt's Knee* and *Bamber's Right Foot*. *Colin's Cheeky Bits* and *Brian Moore's Head* are more profane texts.

Annals: The conventional phrase is *annals of history*, which can be adapted to fit in with specific club *traditions*: 'This one will *go down* in the *annals* of *big European nights* at Anfield'. These *annals* are a mercifully sober alternative to the 'halls of fame', imagined or real, that certain clubs dazzled by American spin are beginning to construct.

Anonymous: Describes a player, generally of star quality, who **disappears** and fails to *produce his form* in a game. The usage requires, of course, that the *anonymous* player is named: 'John Salako was absolutely *anonymous* today'. An alternative is *AWOL*, which can also be used of a specific piece of bad marking: 'Biscan went *AWOL* at that corner'.

Another day: In immediate post-match press conferences, even though the manager is being asked to comment on this particular day, he starts talking about another one: '*On another day* we could have had three or four'; '*On another day* we could have got **something** out of it'. *On their day* is a similar phrase that works to exonerate a team which does not always play to its potential: '*On their day*, Everton can give anyone a game, but they *rolled over* too easily here at St Mary's'.

Anywhere: A common exhortation on the football pitch when you want one of your players to hit *Row Z* rather than trying anything *too clever*. Occasionally, partisan commentators will also let the phrase slip out if a British team is hanging on in the dying minutes: '*Anywhere* will do now, Tony'. In an **almighty scramble**, the words '*could* have *gone anywhere*' are used of the ball once it is safe to assume it will not end up somewhere dangerous.

Aplomb: A goalscorer is said to *finish with aplomb* when it looks as though he knows what he is doing. A finish 'without aplomb' is never remarked upon, but *they all count*.

Aristocrats: Adopted to describe wealthy and famous clubs, without the irony or resentment you might expect of football commentators: 'The ten clubs who have already booked their place read like a *Who's Who* of European football, with fellow *aristocrats*, such as AC Milan and Manchester United, expected to join them'.

Armband: A handy synecdoche for captaincy in journalistic prose: 'With Beckham suspended, Owen will wear the *armband*'. In live commentary, the *armband* can take centre stage in a little moment of drama when the captain is substituted or sent off and nobody can quite remember who should succeed to it.

Armchair fan: Televised football has created the *armchair fan* (he may well be a fan of armchairs, but that's not the main sense), a sedentary species even lower down the scale than the *fair-weather fan*, though neither is quite as annoying as the *nouveau fan*.

Ask: Becoming common as a noun in manager-speak when teams take on a difficult *assignment*: 'To come here and get *something* from the game with our injuries and suspensions was a *big ask*'. There is also a helpful phrase for reporting on an *ambitious* pass to a runner: 'That one from Carl Hoddle *asked a lot* of Gary Bull'. A *woeful* pass *asks* an *awful lot*.

Aspirations: In football journalism teams rarely seem to have title 'dreams' or play-off 'hopes', but usually *aspirations*. These *aspirations* are *tested* when the side in question takes on other aspirants, and *dented* if they lose.

Assemble: Managers who are *rebuilding* their squad, usually through a combination of *wheeling and*

dealing and *nurturing young talent*, should be
described in terms suggestive of Henry Ford: 'Harry's
in the process of *assembling* an excellent side down
there on the South Coast'.

Assist: Ugly neologism minted by the fantasy football industry (perhaps via North American sports
like ice-hockey and basketball) to denote the *contribution* of a player who sets up a goal. The noun is
mandatory, as in 'Alexandersson provided Radzinsky
with an *assist*' rather than 'Alexandersson assisted
Radzinsky'. Available too in Italy, where it looks a
particularly sore thumb: 'Avendo ricevuto un *assist* di
Legrottaglie, Di Vaio ha segnato'. Now even managers
are getting in on the act: 'Steve Bruce should claim an
assist, because only after his bellowing from the
touchline did Morrison move into the box'.

Atmosphere: A noun unthreatened by synonyms
(never say 'ambience'), but, for variety, it can take a
number of different adjectives: *electric*, *red-hot*, *pressure cooker*, *super-charged*, *powder-keg*, *carnival*. In cup
finals players go out on the pitch to *sample* or *soak up*
the *big-match atmosphere* (and to show off their loud
suits). Conversely, a *distinct lack of atmosphere* can be
remarked upon. *Atmosphere* is usually *generated* or
stoked up by home fans.

Attempt on goal: Alternative to *shot* but often used
to emphasise the paucity of shooting chances: 'Baldock
Town barely mustered an *attempt on goal* all afternoon'; '*Attempts on goal* were few and far between in
this dismal *affair*'.

Attentions: A word which conveniently describes the
activity of the close marker: 'Rory Delap kept the ball
under control despite the *attentions* of Leon Clarke'.
The plural seems to suggest a degree of pushiness not

entirely compatible with an attention to the laws of
the game.

Audacious: Likely to refer, on the pitch, to *chips*
or *lobs*. Off the pitch, it may be the club itself that
is seen to be aiming too high: 'Darlington's *audacious swoop* for Asprilla raised some eyebrows this
morning'.

Automatic: 'Delaney has played so well on the right
that he is an *almost automatic* selection'. Note how
the commentator here stops just short of telling the
manager how to do his job – *automatic* is often qualified in this way. Since the introduction of the play-off
system, another usage has evolved: 'Cardiff must be
serious candidates for *automatic promotion*'.

Awareness: The quality shown by players who
know what is *going on around them*: 'Sheringham,
showing great *awareness*, put Shearer in for an unfor-
gettable fourth'. *Great* tends to be the accompanying
adjective for an individual *piece* of *awareness*; *good*
for the quality in general: 'He's got **two feet** and *good
awareness*'.

Away goal: Attracts the adjectives *priceless, all-
important* and *vital*, even if it is far too early in the
tie to know whether it will still have that quality *over
two legs*.

Awkwardly: Categorically the adverb to use in
reporting how a player falls whenever he sustains an
injury in the process: 'McLeod fell *awkwardly* under
challenge by Hall and had to be substituted'.

Axe: 'Their fifth defeat in as many games left Ian
Ross with the *managerial axe* hanging over him'. The
situation is typical enough for the word *managerial* to

be almost redundant, although a manager can also decide to *axe* a player from his team. If *dead men walking* see the writing on the wall they sometimes see fit to *fall on their swords*, but in this report on a *dire **affair*** Bob Cass wheels in another device by which club chairmen can administer the chop: '*Madame Guillotine* still strains against gravity and it remains anybody's guess which of two *managerial heads* will drop into the basket first after a match that was almost comical in its mediocrity'.

Axis: 'The Xabi Alonso/Steven Gerrard *axis* is really beginning to develop'. *Axis* is the fashionable term for a central midfield pairing who *play off* each other. Commentators confronted with two ***inter-passing*** midfielders hailing from Germany and Italy must try not to mention the war.

B

Back four: Established technical term for a defensive ensemble. Add *flat* to distinguish further from a *sweeper system*. The required quality of this unit is *solidity* and its most likely deficiency is to be *caught square*. Although you can talk about the *front two*, midfields are seldom described as a 'middle four': 'France's *midfield quartet* ran the game'.

Back to front: 'It was a pleasing performance against Spurs and the whole team played well from *back to front*'. This programme note does not indicate some daring tactical manoeuvre but reflects a manager's satisfaction in a particularly solid performance by all the units of the side. A modern version, possibly imported from American Football, of the old adage that teams must *build from the back*, available in the senses that long-term success is predicated on a strong defence or that good footballing teams do not play *too long*: 'We said at half time that we had to *build from the back* and the biggest *positive* we got out of the second half was that the *lads* did that and the ball was played through midfield'.

Backheel: Usually *cheeky*, occasionally *adroit, impudent* or *clever*; if it does not *come off*, especially when there were better *options*, *silly* or *stupid*.

Backpass: If worthy of mention, almost invariably *suicidal*. There was of course a period when we were all talking about the *new backpass rule*. It is sobering to think that recent *youth products* have played under this rule all their lives. A particularly *tame* shot may still be derided as *little more than a backpass*, even if the goalkeeper duly picks up the ball with impunity in these circumstances.

Back of the net: Goalscorers are said to *hit*, or *put* the ball *in*, the *back of the net*, and strikers or teams experiencing a goal *drought* cannot *find* the *back of the net*. One of those familiar football clichés which seems to resist deconstruction, given that *anoraks* will point out that the *back of the net* is a target available only to ball-boys with a weak throw. *Net* becomes *netting* only when you hit its sides.

Badge: The noun used in football to designate the coat of arms or insignia of a club. The mercenary attitude of some recent players (Di Canio, Alpay, Lampard *et al.*) previously given to ostentatious displays of loyalty has lent a pejorative colour to the term *badge-kisser*.

Bag: Strikers can *bag* a goal, drawing out the analogy of goalscorer as *poacher*. In plural noun form, a strange but popular unit of measure for *pace, ability* and even *skill*: 'He's got *bags of ability* if only he could use it more consistently'.

Ball: Any pass that is better than average tends to turn into a *ball*: *great ball, what a good through-ball, super ball*. On the other hand, you can bemoan *hopeful balls* into the box. While rugby will use the singular – 'the guys were recycling a lot of ball' – soccer, perhaps less inhibited by potential double entendre, or because possession is less than nine-tenths of the law in the **round-ball** *game*, sticks to the plural: 'Agboola was *pumping* great *balls* into the **mix** all night'. See also **long ball**.

Ballplayer: You'd have thought that any footballer might earn this sobriquet, but it is reserved for the more creative, artistic type. Perhaps more common in the past when *ballplayers* were effete figures threatened by *shoulder-charging, barnstorming, bonecrunching* giants to whom the ball seemed incidental.

Ball-to-hand: What managers say when filing their defence against a penalty **shout** for handball on the grounds that there was no *intent*: 'Jimmy Sirrel felt it was a clear case of *ball-to-hand*'.

Ballwatching: Negligent defenders are admonished with this gerund: 'Dennis was caught *ballwatching* there'. Distinct from 'watching the ball' though this is what it means. One of football's **cardinal sins**.

Banana shot: When we were young, it was possible to say that a dead-ball *specialist* like Rivelino had a particularly *bendy banana*. Nowadays, nobody in Britain seems to call anything swerving round the wall a *banana shot* or *kick*. The term may have fallen into disuse less because of potential double meanings than the memory of *disgraceful* **scenes** where the *banana* was the **missile** thrown at black players. On the other hand, the *inflatable banana* craze of the eighties seemed to pass off without any such connotations.

Banana skin: One of the cherished metaphors elicited by cup-draws: 'So Newcastle must travel to the Bescot. That's a *potential banana skin*, Alan'. It would probably be more accurate to say simply: 'that's *a banana skin*'. Besides, when did you last meet anyone who has slipped on a banana skin?

Bare bones: When a manager moans about his long injury list, usually in anticipation of a defeat, this is the obligatory cliché: 'We **literally** are down to the *bare bones* this time. In all my years in football, I've never known anything like it'. The **spine** may well be missing from what is left of the team's skeleton.

Battle: Military metaphors are endemic to football and the concept of *battling* is habitually used by defiant managers in the **drop zone**: 'We'll keep *battling* away until it's **mathematically** impossible'. *Battles* are enacted all over the pitch, particularly in midfield, and managers often judge a performance in terms of their outcome: 'Graeme Souness admitted, "We lost all the *individual battles* out there. We were outfought and outplayed"'. Note that you are allowed to describe games where violence has been perpetrated by several players on the pitch as a *Battle*. Hence the recent *Battle of Bramall Lane* (when Sheffield United v WBA was abandoned) or the famous *Battle of Santiago* (when *even* an English referee lost control). But never dignify the violence of **so-called fans** by calling it this.

Battle of Britain: Any game whatsoever pitting an English against a Scottish team earns this description. Welsh clubs are exempted, probably because their top three clubs play in the English league. It is an attempt to say that British *bragging rights* are at stake. But it is clumsy. The English and the Scottish fought on the same side in the *Battle of Britain*. And there is a ready selection of tasty Anglo-Scottish battles to choose from. It would however probably be just too delicate to say 'Scholes's second was turning it into a Culloden' or 'Rangers did a Bannockburn over Leeds'. As is characteristic of football parlance, the metaphor exists on condition that its implications remain dormant.

Beautiful game: Phrase used by the sort of people who talk of 'the fair sex'. That is, very few people, though some journalists are given to describing football routinely with these words.

Belief: 'At Highbury Leeds didn't go out and play with any sort of *belief*.' What the Leeds players did not believe in here was their *ability*, or at the very least their *ability to win*. As with *tests of character*, teams are often asked to *show belief* in circumstances where they have every right to play without it.

Bibs and cones: *Bibs* (to differentiate the teams in intra-club five-a-sides) and *cones* (for *dribbling* practice or bleep tests) are two ever-presents on the *training ground*, and they can conveniently describe *coaches* who are thought competent in that setting while not necessarily being considered *manager material*: 'Billy Davies was always well regarded as a *bibs and cones* man, but there were those who expected him to struggle at Deepdale'.

Big boys: 'Oldham *hit back* in style to teach Brian Talbot's newly promoted Rushden side a *harsh* early *lesson* about life with the *big boys* in Division Two'. It seems whenever teams go up a division they have to adjust to an initial size disadvantage. The third round of the FA Cup is also always notable for the entrance of the *big boys*. When a beating is being duly administered, the *big boys* turn into *men against boys*.

Big match: Like the *match of the day*, once an innocuous way of describing a *heavyweight **clash*** or ***plum tie***. But, just like *match of the day*, a phrase removed from the language of football by the television programme that enshrined it.

Big time: 'Wright and Bright were excellent strikers, but both seemed *big time* to me'; 'If the senior players are *cliquish* and *big time*, that will affect the ***set-up*** right down the line to the apprentices'. True to their typical backgrounds, footballers are suspicious of those who get ideas above their station and have therefore adopted the sarcastic showbiz expression with relish. The *big stage* has no such negative connotations and is somewhere players always want to *shine*.

Bit-part: 'Nyarko spent a season on loan at Monaco and another at PSG before playing a *bit-part* at Goodison in the last campaign'; 'Ellison has played only a *bit-part* role since joining from Chester in January'. This term, indicating a *fringe player* rather than a front-liner, seems to be used far more of footballers than actors.

Blast: As a verb, what managers do to chide and *berate* their players, perhaps if one of them has *blasted* a shot *wildly over*. As a noun, used to register the fact that the referee has stopped play: 'Loud *blast* from referee Winter' means he has blown his whistle rather than his top. A hallmark of Bill McLaren, but used by football commentators also.

Blatant: A common qualifier, whatever the degree of the offence. Used particularly of *handball*, *timewasting* and *shirtpulling*.

Blend: Always seems to be of *youth and experience*.

Blinder: A *blinder* is played by a pre-eminent player, usually, though not always, an opposition goalkeeper when on defiantly good form: 'We should have finished them off, but Thomas Myhre had a *blinder*'. Used more by footballers themselves than by journalists. Perhaps strangely, also used of referees, despite the fact that one of the most tired terrace witticisms is to direct the **officials** to the nearest opticians. The opposite is *shocker* or **stinker**.

Block: Players are said to *block* shots more than they *block* opponents. But *block off* describes the action of a defender you will see in every game where he **shepherds** a ball to safety while getting in the way of an attacker. Records either a legitimate piece of defending – 'Delap *blocked* Scowcroft *off* cleverly there' – or a less savoury version: 'Keegan was *blocked off* very **cynically** by Tardelli'.

Blow wide open: Occasionally used of a *defence-splitting pass*, but more commonly employed to describe a result which revives a team's **aspirations**: 'Newcastle's win has *blown* the title race *wide open*'.

Blue: Fans of teams that wear *blue* tend to rejoice by singing songs not written for happy people: '*Blue* Moon, I saw you standing alone'; 'I never felt more like singing the *blues*'. The rhyme with *lose* may have encouraged the impression that teams in red always have the upper hand but times are changing.

Blushes: Seem to be referred to in football only when
they have been *spared*, usually those of a higher division team given a *scare* in the cup: 'Dave Jones
blasted the attitude of his Wolves players after Alex
Rae's late *leveller spared* their *blushes*'.

Bobbly: Adjective for corrugated pitches, inspired
more by the way a football behaves on such surfaces.
The corresponding verb is suggested also by the com-
plicity of the goalkeeper in this next example:
'Davison *thrashed* only at the Lancashire air, and the
ball *bobbled* mockingly over his foot.'

Bodies: Men tend to become *bodies* in two particular
situations: *in the box* and *behind the ball*. In both cases,
it seems, the presence in itself of these *bodies* could be
important (by providing a telling deflection or making
a fortuitous *block*) irrespective of human will or
intention. *Shirts* have the same implicit powers.

Bonus ball: 'Anything we take from *places* like Old
Trafford and Stamford Bridge will be a *bonus ball*'.
Now that the *Premiership* has become like the SPL,
managers of clubs outside the *magic circle* are sometimes not even asking their players to *show belief*,
but hoping to win something in the lottery before
concentrating on the *must-win* fixtures.

Bony: Less common in the era of undersoil heating
but used of a typical mid-season pitch where the frost
has barely come out of the ground.

Boo-boys: Those fans that barrack or *get on the back*
of their own players. They seem to embarrass journalists, who think it rather churlish to disapprove of
any player in club *colours*, hence both the specificity
and the condescension in the term *boo-boys*, as
though good ordinary mature fans would not boo a

player. Even when, quite patently, a whole stadium is doing so, the term *boo-boys* works to maintain the impression that it is the action of a *tiny minority* habitually given to this kind of behaviour. Comment-ators invariably itch to describe the moment of skill or, better still, the goal by the reviled player that will *silence* the *boo-boys*, the first stage in *winning them over*.

Bookable offence: A second *bookable offence* is often abbreviated to *second bookable*, in the same way that a second yellow card is abbreviated to *second yellow*: 'Dugarry went off after a *second bookable*'.

Boost: Place the adjectives *massive* or *much-needed* before this word, when describing a player returning from an *injury layoff*, or a victory that has **kick-started** your season.

Boot: To hit the ball without much or indeed any fin-esse. Players who *boot*, *belt*, *hoof*, or, better still, *leather* it choose *safety first* or the *Row Z* option.

Bore draw: Fairly laboured term for a scoreless draw, driven by the rhyme, which seems to have eclipsed the *dour midfield struggle*. Conversely, a blank **score-line** where both keepers have been kept busy is men-tioned in despatches as 'by no means *your typical nil-nil*'.

Bosman: Immortal, invisible, ubiquitous, Jean-Marc Bosman must be the most famous mediocre player in the history of the game (unless you're Scottish and prefer Costa Rica's Cayasso). But Bosman has got a whole eponym to himself, as in *on a Bosman*.

Bouncebackability: Advertisers are quick to hitch a ride on the sporting bandwagon. Endowed to the lexicon by Iain Dowie, and popularised by Soccer AM, *bouncebackability* has now featured in an ad for mattresses which presumably sag a little less than Crystal Palace have.

Bow out: The requisite verb to set up a reference to a team departing at a certain stage in the Cup. Another of those terms that makes the FA Challenge Cup seem considerably more polite and olde-worldy than all other competitions.

Box-to-box: 'Caminero shows such consistency from *box-to-box*'. This is not a review from *Cigar Monthly* but a characteristic tribute to a player whose *engine* allows him to *arrive* in the opponents' penalty area and *track back* to help his own defenders.

Boys: Less common than *lads* but immortalised in Mick Channon's eulogies of *the boy Lineker* (pronounced to rhyme with 'wine acre') and Graham Taylor's tautologies involving *young boys*: 'Shearer, Palmer, Batty – they're all *young boys* and they've done ever so well today'. See also *boo-boys* and *big boys*.

Bragging rights: Increasingly common cliché employed in the build-up to *derby* games: 'The *blue half* of the city hopes to have *bragging rights,* as was the case last year'. Cities are divided neatly in half in these circumstances, even when the *fan-base* is not distributed as evenly.

Brains trust: Used occasionally in live commentary to describe a collection of players standing over a *dead-ball* **situation**: 'Roberto Carlos, Beckham and Zidane are the *brains trust* for this one'. The implication is that they are deciding which *well-worked* move *straight off* the *training ground* they should deploy, whereas they are more likely arguing about who is going to *have a crack*.

Brawl: If *handbags* should escalate into full-blown fisticuffs, this is almost invariably described as a *brawl*. The superlative case is a *22-man brawl*, although goalkeepers rarely run *all of* fifty yards to get involved. Perhaps because the game has many metaphors of *battle* and fighting to describe legitimate aggression, a real fist-fight is associated with the bar-room.

Bread and butter: After glamorous midweek exploits in Europe, it's always back to the *bread and butter* of *domestic* competition. Also used of teams returning from cup distractions to the routine of league matches. The image neatly conveys the reassuring rhythm of the league programme. As long as teams remain in a cup tournament, the league is *bread and butter*, but, once they are eliminated, it is something worth *concentrating* on: 'Back in the *bread-and-butter* world of the league this was a performance with jam on it'.

Brigade: Seen in recent years as a collective noun for particular sub-sets of football supporters. At either end of the scale, you may currently find the *Prawn Sandwich Brigade* (described as such by Roy Keane) and the *Burberry Brigade*. The latter are more likely than the former to join up with the *travelling army*.

Build-up: Tends to take the adjective *patient*. *Build-up play* is often revered as a *continental* characteristic in contrast to the more *direct* English *game*.

Bulge: Nets do this when they welcome the ball: 'Breitner looked up, *let fly*, the net *bulged*'. A paratactic

way of reporting a goal, if you want to convey the
speed with which the events leading up to it occured.
Compare: 'Ferguson *slid in* ahead of his marker and a
moment later the Birmingham net was *billowing*'.

Bullet: 'It was a *bullet-header* from Katschuro'. It is
only headers which seem to attract this compound
form and the related verb: 'Plymouth's unmarked
Mickey Evans *bulleted* a header wide from five yards'.
However, when players are said to *pull the trigger*, the
metaphor denotes the action of a footballer about to
kick not head the ball, often presaging a crucial and
timely *intervention* by a defender.

Bundle: The likely term for reporting on an untidy
or scrambled goal, when it is not always clear which
part of whose *anatomy applied* the final touch:
'Nolan will try and claim Bolton's *bundled* goal in
the ninetieth minute'. While the ball is most often
bundled in or *bundled over* the line, it may also be
wastefully *bundled wide* or hurriedly *bundled away*
by a defender or goalkeeper. A *good **old-fashioned***
English forward would once be intent on *bundling*
both goalkeeper and ball *over* the line, but this was
always going to be too *physical* an approach for
Europe's liking, even if it is still attempted and occasionally permitted: 'Lehmann was later *bundled into*
the net, along with the ball, by Leon Mckenzie'; 'A
goal four minutes from time by Stuart Bamford after
Michael Kalli was *bundled over* was allowed to stand
by ref Mike Johnson despite the Harlow *stopper* lying
injured on the ground'.

Bury: Provides an effective way of registering an
emphatic strike: 'Davies *buried* a low shot past Edwin
van der Sar'. Others make sure that if they can't *bury*
it low, they *bury* it deep: 'Rooney *buried* a volley in
Schwarzer's *rigging* with a thunderous first-time

strike'. In the hyperbole of yesteryear this would have amounted to *bursting the net*. But there are times when the hyperbole amounts almost to what it says, for, in the words of his manager, Rooney 'doesn't do *tap-ins*'.

Busier of the keepers: A phrase used to assess the balance of the play when the score is level or a match has been drawn. Serviceable among careful commentators who wish to imply, but not to say frankly, that one team was much better than the other: 'Vale and City fought out a scrappy **stalemate**, but Musselwhite was much the *busier of the keepers*'.

Busy: The adjective *busy* is reserved for midfielders, usually breathless, talentless, **pint-sized** ones. In midweek results **round-ups**, announcers often talk about a *busy night of football*, perhaps a quiet warning to people waiting for the weather forecast that there are more results than they might expect.

Buzz: This is noticed *about the place*, be it the football club, the ground or the whole town, before or after a significant achievement. Often the *buzz* is remarked upon, perhaps as *audible* or even *tangible*, in the build-up to a *massive* game, especially in the cup. But it can also linger in the atmosphere after the particular upset has been achieved: 'There's a *real buzz* about the training ground after Saturday's cup win'; 'Some 3,600 people saw Weymouth beat newly-relegated Lincoln 3–0, and the *whole town* was *buzzing*'.

C

Calling card: The euphemism for a heavy challenge **early** *doors* to let your opponent know who you are. The Big-Ronism was *reducer*. Paul Scholes was once told just before an England v Sweden match by manager Kevin Keegan to *drop a grenade in there*. Scholes was booked within one minute for a *mistimed* tackle and later sent off for a *second yellow*.

Cameras: *One for the cameras* is a save or *dive* that is deemed unnecessarily *theatrical*. Players or teams are sometimes described as having a good record *in front of the cameras*, suggesting they are *fancy* Dans who only give *one hundred per cent* when the world is watching.

Capable: The word adopted by commentators, often notched up to *well capable*, to warn of a player's skills at a dead-ball *situation*: 'We all know what John Sheridan is *capable* of *from here*'. That the free kick is within his range of capability may also be indicated by the information that 'this is John Sheridan *territory*'.

Capitalise: In football, seen in the phrase *failed to capitalise on,* whether it be a lead, a period of dominance, the greater possession, the wind at your back or some other advantage. If you do *capitalise*, you rarely say so in these words. Rather, you *make it count* or *translate* your superiority *into goals*.

Capture: Used as a noun more than a verb in the context of transfers: 'Their recent £2.5m *capture* from Leicester did the damage'. Form is always *recaptured* when it has been lost, but never 'captured' when it is found in the first place.

Carbon copy: Despite the advent of the word processor, still the figure for goals or incidents that repeat themselves in a match: 'Three minutes later Leonhardsen scored a *carbon copy* of his first goal'. See also *sixpence, slide rule, woodwork*.

Cardinal sins: In St Augustine, among other Doctors of the Church, the seven deadly sins are: pride, greed, lust, envy, gluttony, anger and sloth. At St Andrews or at St James's, among other grounds, the footballing *cardinal sins* are: passing the ball across your own penalty area, **showboating**, making a substitution just before a set piece against you, **ballwatching**, not playing to the whistle, not **organising** the wall and not giving your team-mates a **shout**.

Career-ending: Describes a very bad challenge: 'That could have been a *career-ending* tackle from Dicks'. As soon as the possibility becomes real, commentators are far too polite to say so but come up with some platitude, while the stretcher is coming out, such as: 'You have to hope that isn't as *bad* as it *first looks*'.

Caretaker: Whether used on its own or in the compound noun *caretaker-manager*, this is standard form for designating a temporary or stand-in boss. In order to avoid confusing him with the man who locks the ground up (and confusing them both), the speaker may take care to say that 'Jimmy Gabriel has been appointed *in a caretaking capacity*'.

Cash-strapped: The favoured adjective for clubs in *financial difficulties*: '*Cash-strapped* Clarets put a *dismal* run behind them to set up a *money-spinning* tie to ease their financial worries'.

Catenaccio: Italian for *doorbolt*, used to define a *defensive-minded* system of football with a *stopper* at the back. A connoisseur of Europe in the mould of El Tel might introduce such a technical term into his discourse for a little glamour, at the same time remembering to put it on the shortlist for the name of the themed bar and restaurant he might be opening inside the new **Wembley**.

Cats: On account of their natural agility or a taste for stand-offish detachment, goalkeepers and only goal-keepers may be labelled *feline*. But there have been but few if any *cats* as such since Lev Yashin and Peter Bonetti. Perhaps this is because of the modern emphasis on a goalkeeper's ***distribution***.

Caught cold: A phrase imported from boxing naturally applicable to teams who get off to the *worst possible start*: 'The Grecians were *caught cold* from the first set piece of the match'. If a team is *caught on the break* later in the game, you may use another pugilistic metaphor: 'Christian Gross was left in despair after a *classic sucker punch* by City'.

Cauldron: Whether through the advent of genteel all-seater stadia or the invention of the microwave oven, *cauldron* no longer seems to be the metaphor reserved for depicting crowds that are large and hostile. *Pressure cookers* also seem to have gone out of fashion (see ***atmosphere***).

Cause: An attempt at getting three points or at progressing to the next round may take on the proportions of an epic quest, a heroic struggle. The noun *cause* comes in handy, particularly when this quest was in vain: 'I can't fault my players – they gave everything *to the cause*'; 'Etcheverria did not help the Bolivians' *cause* by getting himself sent off within minutes'. In both statements, the removal of the words in italics would perhaps compromise dignity more than meaning.

Caution: *Caution* is indeed required, because yellow-brandishing refs say something like: 'Any more of that and you'll get a red'. But it is probably a bit old-fashioned now that the yellow card has itself become a form of punishment (rather than just a warning of possible future punishment), leading of itself, in some circumstances, to a subsequent ban. Hence the foot-balling equivalent to walking on eggs is to be *on a yellow* during a tournament. At a pre-season friendly in America, we once heard this come over the tannoy: 'A yellow *caution* card has been *administered* by the referee'.

Celebrations: When a ***perfectly good goal*** is disal-lowed by a linesman's unsuspected or late flag, *cele-brations*, encompassing both the joy of fans and the increasingly choreographed reactions of the goal-scorer, are *cut short* (or sometimes *stifled*). If, within, say, five minutes after a goal, the opposition **hits back** with one of its own, the *celebrations* should instead be described as *short-lived*.

Centre-forward: Available adjectives include *barn-storming*, *burly*, *bustling*, *rumbustious*, *swashbuckling*. These qualities are implicit in the more general stereotype of the ***old-fashioned***, physical, British *centre-forward*. *Number nine* is still an acceptable if outdated synonym.

Challenge: Sounds rather noble. Indeed, the noun is used as often for attempts to win the ball *cleanly* as for *heavy challenges* which may constitute a foul (*dirty* is a word which sticks to *player* and *tackle* much more than *challenge*). Just as an ***effort*** in foot-ball can mean a goal as well as an **attempt on goal**, so a *challenge* is a tackle rather than, as you might think, a prelude to such a tackle.

Champagne: Although some of its ***characters*** have been partial to a magnum or two, the professional game tends to get no kicks from *champagne*: 'Berkovic is a *champagne player* and doesn't like it up him'. *Champagne football* tends to be for **aristocrats** – less fashionable clubs can find the **big time** goes to their heads: 'Now Norwich have *tasted the champagne*, they don't like the lager'.

Champions League: 'You're having a laugh'. It is properly neither for champions nor a league, but these two English words have carried it round Europe, to the strains of that awful sub-Handelian anthem. It does not generate a vocabulary of its own like the FA Cup, though plenty of commentators and journalists refer to the *Champions League circus*. This is a neat way of saying that the competition is undeniably spectacular and entertaining, but contrived. The UEFA Cup can now be described as little more than a *distraction* while, worst of all, there will be no more European Cup Winners Cup winners.

Change: *Make a change* is used particularly by pundits recommending a substitution which they consider overdue: 'It really is time Mick McCarthy *made a change*'. Managers are said, with inevitable disregard for campanology, to *ring the changes* when making a multiple substitution or a large number of close-season signings.

Channel: Coaches are forever exhorting their charges to knock it *into* or *down* the *channels*, although it is not always exactly clear where these *channels* are. The received wisdom is that it is *in behind the full-backs* where tireless forwards *run the channels*. But midfielders can also operate **up and down** the *inside-left* or *inside-right channels*. At any rate, getting it into the *channels* is the same as getting it into *good areas*.

Character: Used in particular when British clubs concede an early goal in Europe. When a summariser says that this will be a *test of character* the implication is that the team tested will get beaten. A reference to *characters in the dressing room* can also emphasise the resilient qualities of certain players, but is more likely to tell apart those players who *enjoy a laugh*. See **quality** for another example of singular and plural having different shades of meaning.

Chase the game: Teams trying to get back on level terms can find themselves *chasing the game*. The phrase is then likely to emerge from the manager concerned as a rueful reflection on *gaps* left at the back, rather than as a tactical instruction on the best ways to *get forward*: 'We paid the price for having to *chase the game* for too long'.

Chasing pack: The standard description of clubs with title **aspirations** who find themselves behind a leading team. Almost a misleading image insofar as it might suggest that these teams are collaborating as they hunt down the leader. But the results **round-up** may prove that they can *do each other a favour*.

Chequebook: 'After brandishing his *chequebook* all season, Malcolm Allison is expected to get results'; 'Sammy Chung will be reaching for the *chequebook* again this summer'. A *chequebook manager* enjoys a reputation for lavish expenditure and is unlikely also to be a **tracksuit manager**. Football parlance would have you believe that the *chequebook* remains the method by which multi-million pound transfers are paid. It will be interesting to see whether it stands its ground like **slide rules** and **sixpence** pieces, in their anachronistic splendour, or whether it will be supplanted by references to credit facilities and BACS transfers.

Chip: *Chips* would seem to be the same as *lobs*, though the latter are more likely to involve – or can *take out* – a goalkeeper. The noun takes a variety of adjectives: *delicate, exquisite* or even *delicious*; **ambitious**, **audacious** or *cheeky* if executed from long distance.

Chocolate wrist: This appears when a goalkeeper *gets down* to a shot but can only *parry* it into the net: 'It has to be said there was a bit of a *chocolate wrist* from David on their second goal'. Therefore the opposite of a ***strong hand***. In the case of outfield players prone to similar gaffes, the brand of confectionery can be narrowed down as the shot goes wide: 'Dario Silva, the Uruguay veteran, exhibited a finishing style that made one think of *Toblerone boots* and Geoff Thomas's England career'.

Clash: It is always a *top-of-the-table clash*, but a *relegation scrap*, ***battle*** or, when it gets really ***ugly***, *dogfight*. The *clash*, sometimes of *heavyweights* or *Titans*, sounds more heroic, but this doesn't mean it can't turn out ***scrappy*** in the actual event: 'This *drab clash* had end of season written all the way through it'. Even in the days of the ***computer***, it is not always possible to avoid a *clash* of fixtures.

Class: As in other sports, *class* usually *tells in the end*. When their team is winning handsomely, fans may taunt their opposite numbers by singing the question 'What's it like to be *outclassed*?' It gains impact and some sort of social dimension if *outclassed* is directed with a northern short vowel to southern fans or sung with the longer southern vowel to northerners. There is perhaps a reflection of the northern music halls in *class act*, an expression reserved for an individual player rather than a *collective unit*. A popular touch, too, in the predilection of certain football managers for saying a player is *different class* when commenting on a ***complete package***. It seems that the alliteration offered by *classy* in conjunction with the names of some players, *classy Klas Ingesson* for one, spares them the trouble of having to be it.

Clatter: This verb is mandatory whenever a player has an unexpected encounter with advertising hoardings. Also describes *robust* tackles, especially from behind: 'Huddlestone *clattered* Sutton again there'.

Claw: When a team has *restored **parity*** more by an act of will than by particularly outstanding play, they are described as having *clawed their way back* into the match. The other team, meanwhile, will have been *pegged back*. Goalkeepers tend to *claw* or *paw* away the ball when bringing a particularly **strong** hand to bear in *last-ditch* circumstances: 'Tony Capaldi held his head in disbelief when his 25-yard volley was *clawed out* of the top-corner by Camp'.

Clean sheet: This goes down to the credit of the goal-keeper and his defenders, but the modern manager is always ready to assume responsibility: 'I'd have liked all three points, but I'm pleased with the *clean sheet*'. An accumulation of *clean sheets*, known more austerely as *shut-outs*, soon begins to take on statistical significance: 'The goalless draw on Saturday was Bolton's fifth *shut-out* in six matches'. But not the sort of thing a striker wants to take up space in his **locker**: 'Crouch has rather too many *clean sheets* of his own'.

Clear-the-air talks: When players are *unsettled* they never simply meet their manager in order 'to clear the air', but have to hold *clear-the-air talks*. The presence of agents may be implied.

Climb: Players may be said to *climb off the bench*, a phrase not really warranted by the height of said bench, but note: 'Little Jamie Forrester *climbed off the bench* to make it five wins in a row for Hull'. When a player is penalised for fouling another as they *compete* for a header, the offender is said to *climb all over him*.

Clinical: The definitive word for the most defini-tive act in football. A way of distinguishing Thierry Henry as a *finisher* from your average *practitioner*. No doubt Arsène Wenger would conceive of a **trademark** Henry goal not as *clinical* but *chirurgical*.

Clip: Alternative to *shoot*, usually when the ball goes just over the bar: 'Moussa Saib ran to meet the near-post cross but *clipped* it narrowly over the bar'. The ball itself can *clip* or *shave* the **woodwork**, or miss by *a coat of paint*.

Clog: 'You had to get respect in the sense that people could not *clog* you without knowing that they would be *clogged* back'. John Giles is the source for this quotation, which features a euphemism for **kick** not nearly as common today. But for those with long memories or Lowry copies in their house, it remains a viable word to describe roughhouse play. *Clogger* is the related noun for the kind of player who *puts himself about* because he cannot *make the ball his friend*.

Close down: Used regularly of outfield players to indicate what Italians call *il pressing* (not, inciden-tally, to be confused with the identical French word for dry-cleaning). The phrase can also refer to the action of an advancing goalkeeper: 'It was a good chance but Myhill *closed down the angle* quickly'. The geometry here is mostly in the commentator's mind, since this is a **regulation** save unless the keeper really **made himself big**.

Club versus country debate: References to such a *debate* would be more appropriate in Australia or Uruguay, all of whose best players *ply* their **trade** abroad, yet whenever Premiership managers begrudge a player *international* **duty** or there are *late withdrawals* from an England squad, allusions to this interminable but usually inaudible *debate* surface.

Coach and horses: What you can proverbially drive through a defence once it has been opened up by either a **killer ball** or its own **schoolboy** incompetence.

Collectively: Whereas a manager laments the loss of *individual* **battles** or the proliferation of *individual mistakes*, he is unlikely to *single out* individuals after a win but praise the way his players defended *collectively as a unit*.

Collector's item: When goals come from an *unlikely source* they can be designated in this way (or classified as a *museum piece*): 'The goal from Jeff Kenna, his first in Birmingham *colours*, was a *real collector's item*'. When a player scores in untypical fashion, there is another possibility: 'The *rare headed goal* from Brooking was *one for the scrapbook* in more ways than one'.

Colossus: Reserved for players who perform *head and shoulders* above their team-mates. You would expect the adjective to be used of centre-halves and forwards but in fact the position seems irrelevant: 'Inspired by the midfield *colossus* that is Steven Gerrard, Liverpool brushed aside modest visitors'.

Colours: A word used when counting up appearances in a particular **shirt**: 'It's only his third home outing in Standard Liège *colours*'. But the word *colours* has come to denote the replica **strip** or *kit* worn by fans. Mildly pejorative, it is often to be seen in the phrase *No Football Colours* on the doors of wine bars and other establishments of high repute. The **hooligan** slogan 'these *colours* never run', thanks to the little pun, is more amusing than menacing.

Come-and-get-me plea: 'Arsenal's Cygan *issues* a *come-and-get-me plea* to Lille'; 'Lille defender Stathis Tavlaridis has *issued* a *come-and-get-me plea* to Rangers'. These pleas are always *issued* in the tabloids and always seem to take this hyphenated form. Perhaps the wording arises because those desperate for a move know that clubs are said to *come in* for a player and that, in order to attract their *interest*, you should not play too hard to get. We have yet to see an article where an *unsettled* player exclusively tells the *Sunday People* that 'it would be quite nice if someone made a bid but there's no rush because I haven't put my house on the market yet'. The response of the player's current employer to a *come-and-get-me plea* is to issue their own equally dramatic *hands-off warning*. If that doesn't work, the club (or the sub-editor of the paper through which negotiations are being informally conducted) will *slap* a *not-for-sale sign* on their man.

Come through: First-team **regulars** who have been out injured usually *prove* their fitness by *coming through* a reserve fixture. Teams with *Academies* can also boast of young talent *coming through*. And once these **starlets** have indeed *come through the ranks*, they are then ready to *emerge*, a term possibly applied more on the international *stage*: 'Portugal's *emerging* youngsters make them **many people's idea** of the tournament winners'.

Come to the boil: The culinary metaphor seems right for Italy, *notorious slow-starters*, who *come to the boil* later on in tournaments, unless anything Korean is thrown into the mix. A match may itself be *simmering nicely*, only for it to *boil over* into something *unsavoury*. See also **cauldron**.

Comfort zone: Some definable point in the modern game where any goal by the opposition would be a *consolation* rather than a *lifeline*: 'Once in the *comfort zone*, Ferguson took off Scholes and Giggs to preserve some energy for Wednesday's vital Champions League *clash* against Stuttgart'.

Command: Tends to be used of goalkeepers (as opposed to mere *shotstoppers*) who *come for crosses* and *command their areas*, or centre-halves who are a *commanding presence* at the back. Players in any position, if they are rated highly enough, can *command* a certain transfer fee.

Compact: Used of grounds, as a polite way of saying 'small', although perhaps implying a compliment to the fervour of the home fans (*quaint* tends to suggest a ground which is falling down but *full of character*). A defensive-minded coach can praise his team for being *nice and compact* if they have prevented the game from becoming *stretched*.

Competition: A striker's tally for the season is sometimes counted *in all competitions*, to distinguish this figure from the league only. Even including the Inter-Toto and Auto Windscreens Cups there aren't in fact that many competitions. *Competition for places* is usually a good thing (see also *selection headache*). Whether a player returning from injury has played in friendlies *behind closed doors* or for the reserves, his re-appearance in the first team is always described as his *first competitive action* since the injury.

Complete package: 'Andy Cole's the *complete package*: pace, power and poise.' Manager-speak formula of praise similar to *class act* but susceptible to hedging. Barry Fry's description of Ruud van Nistelrooy as '*near enough* the most *complete* player' ignores the complication that completeness does not admit of degrees.

Completely: The kind of overemphatic adverb beloved of commentators in phrases such as *completely anonymous*, *bamboozled*, *out of position*, *wrong-footed*. The most common of all is *completely unmarked*, usually deployed with a touch of self-righteousness: 'The El Salvador defence have left Kiss *completely unmarked* for the second time in a matter of minutes'. *Comprehensively* may sound more comprehensive if a goalkeeper is beaten *all ends up* or a team *outplayed*.

Complexion: Any key incident seems to *change* the *complexion* of the game instantaneously: 'That miss changed the *whole complexion* of the game'; 'The *complexion* of the game changed **completely** when Smith was sent off'.

Composure: Usually implicit here is a situation *in front of goal*, although the word can be used of defenders, goalkeepers or *firebrands* also. *Composure* is *shown* or *kept* in football parlance, whereas *discipline* is what you tend to *lose*.

Compound: As we near the end of a match report, this word always goes with *misery* (unless there are other alliterative possibilities) when an injury or sending-off afflicts the losing side: 'Thistle's *torment* was *compounded* when Derek Fleming was shown a red card for a tussle with Pars substitute Noel Hunt'.

Computer: The *computer* responsible for the fixture list may be attributed powers of irony that can be quirky or downright vindictive, as when it pairs a manager with his former club on the first day of the season or *throws up* successive fixtures against Champions League participants. See also **sink in**.

Concentrate on the league: Many years ago a manager must have said this in all seriousness after *crashing out* of the Cup, but today it tends to be recited with heavy irony: 'At least we can "*concentrate on the league*" now'. Teams involved in cup tournaments, as well as the ***bread and butter*** of the league, are said, a bit prosaically, to be playing on *different fronts*. But this image is nowhere near as good as the German phrase in which such teams are said to be *dancing at three weddings*. In 2002 Bayer 'Neverkusen' were eventually guests at three funerals.

Conditions: Describes weather, terrain or the effect the former has on the latter: *blustery conditions, awful conditions, perfect conditions*. Add *for football* to all these expressions, according to taste. Allusion is sometimes made to *underfoot conditions*, but less so than in racing or rugby.

Consolation: Defines a late goal scored by the losing team. So definitively, in fact, that the word *goal* can be dispensed with: 'Bowles got a late *consolation* for QPR'. The diminishing degrees of consolation in our further examples suggest the word has otherwise become a quasi-technical term: 'Darcheville's strike was little more than a late *consolation*'; 'Kowenicki's late ***effort*** brought no *consolation*'. Note that the noun, one of many ossified terms in football, is preferred to the verb 'to console', usage of which would risk restoring the actual meaning to the word.

Contact: When decisions are *hotly **disputed***, the main ***talking point*** is often whether *contact* has been *made*: 'Although there appeared to be *minimal contact*, Huckerby stayed down'. Had Huckerby *stayed on his feet* to shoot, he might have *made* a *good contact* or *got* a *good connection*.

Contest: Not used much in football as a synonym for *match* (***affair*** or ***clash*** are preferred) but when a goal puts a game beyond doubt it is very common for a commentator to look at his watch and pronounce that it's *all over as a contest*. The *as a contest* does not add very much (compare ***ruined as a spectacle***) except to convey that he thinks the losing team have stopped trying or might as well stop. There is no equivalent ready-made expression when a club sees its season end prematurely after a Cup *exit* and it does not even need to ***concentrate on the league***. But it is possible to say: 'Tottenham's season is now *effectively* over'.

Contribution: Managers are fond of this word either to encourage strikers who cannot find the net – 'All Neil Shipperley needs is a goal as his *all-round contribution* is first class' – or to emphasise that there is much more to their strikers than a ***poacher***'s instinct: 'Alexander deserved the goal for his *overall contribution*'.

Contrive: Most common in the phrase: 'Milosevic *contrived* to miss when it would have been ***easier to score***'. In other contexts, the verb is used when there seems to be minimal contrivance as in: 'Somehow George Berry *contrived* to deflect the ball into his own net'; 'From 2-0 up, Bury *contrived* to throw the game away'.

Corinthian: *Corinthian* Casuals is a football club renowned for its commitment to the amateur ethos – team spirit, humble aspiration and selfless solidarity. These values have been seamlessly transferred to our new national stadium, as advertised on its website: 'The *Corinthian* Club is set to redefine the ***Wembley*** experience. Located on the first floor concourse, and with direct access to the *Corinthian* seats, this elegant restaurant will offer an unprecedented quality of dining. And whether you entertain on a large scale or prefer a more intimate setting, the *Corinthian* Restaurant provides the perfect environment for socialising or networking'.

Courtesy of: Tired alternative for 'as a result of':
'Preston secured the win *courtesy of* a *brace* of goals by
Fuller'. More ironically applied, it would seem, in the
following example: 'Giggs increased Man United's
advantage *courtesy of* a poor backpass by Bergsson'. *By
virtue of* is a close cousin.

Covered: Whenever we are told that the keeper *had
it covered* we infer that, if a save had been required, he
would have made it. The typical situations, therefore,
are after the ball has *fizzed* narrowly wide or hit the
woodwork: 'It's just *shaved* the post but I think Porter
had that *one covered*'. Never say 'the keeper had covered that one'.

Credit: Given in a generous or patronising way by
managers in victory or defeat: 'All *credit* to Leicester,
they **completely** *outbattled* us today'; 'Give them a lot
of *credit*, they kept on *battling* for 90 minutes'. An
alternative is: 'You've got to *hand* it to them'. Commentators, too, will give due *credit* to a team for their
effort under pressure, if they are in the lead and
refuse to *sit back*, or if they are well behind and refuse
to *lie down*.

Cricket score: When one side is administering a real
drubbing, and certainly once they have *hit* the other
team *for six*, they are said to be in danger of *running
up* a *cricket score*. The videprinter also recognises the
improbable nature of the tally by spelling it out in
capitals: 'St Mirren 7 (SEVEN) Brechin City 1'.
Presumably, rain would have stopped play for 7–1 to
be a real cricket score at the close.

Cross the park: Or, more precisely, to cross Stanley
Park; in other words to move from Everton to Liver-
pool or vice versa: 'Since Barmby *crossed the park*,
Everton have lacked an attacking midfielder'. Standard

in *Liverpool Echo* prose. You can *cross the river* in some cities, or the car park in Dundee.

Cross-cum-shot: 'Blackpool were *breaking* in waves and Coid became the next to threaten with a *cross-cum-shot* which improbably *bobbled* through the six-yard box and out of play'. Impossible to say in a case like this if the player knew any better than the reporter whether the precise intention was a centre ***drilled in*** to the box or an ***effort*** on goal.

Crowded: Typically, if anybody is remotely in the line of the keeper's vision during an ***almighty*** *scramble*, the penalty area is described as *crowded*. The Big-Ronism was *crowd scene*.

Cruyff turn: One of the very few examples in football where an individual has lent his name to a particular *piece of business*. The *Higuita scorpion* is rare but not extinct, while some players with particularly refined *simulation* techniques may now have a *Fosbury flop* in their ***locker*** of tricks. Cruyff junior, who preferred commentators to call him Jordi, modestly did not want to be confused with the genius who patented the turn, or maybe was just worried that people would expect him to be capable of performing at will a move which is usually ***sublime*** but sometimes ridiculous: 'Traore's "*Cruyff Turn*" into his own net condemned Liverpool to a premature FA Cup exit'.

Cup final: In football parlance all *must-win* games now seem to have turned into *cup finals*. Managers threatened by relegation, haunted by the ***axe***, declare: 'Every game from now till the end of the season is a *cup final*'. Condescending fans of big teams, particularly Manchester United supporters, taunt the support of smaller clubs when they meet in a match by singing: 'One-nil in your *cup final*'. The FA *Cup Final* remains the reference point for a match that really counts, although, to all intents and purposes, it now matters less to the **PLC** than a Champions League qualifier against Skonto Riga.

Curl: Denotes *bend* on the ball, as in 'Gallas *curled* a spectacular shot around Paul Robinson'. When it comes to the noun, *curler* is preferred to 'bender'.

Cushion: Whereas rugby commentators identify the gap between teams as being 'within a score' or not, football observers prefer to talk of the *cushion* that is, or would be, an additional goal, a goal which would *surely*, *effectively*, put the game beyond reach. Leading teams may enjoy a six-point *cushion* over the **chasing pack**. Headers and lay-offs can also be *cushioned*, particularly if they set up an *inviting* chance.

Custodian: Staple synonym always available for *goalkeeper*. Likely to be used with a degree of wry self-consciousness these days: 'Ferguson is almost certain to *offload* one of his *calamitous custodians* in the summer'.

Cutting edge: The readily applied cliché for teams who play **pretty** *triangles* but lack something in the **final** *third*: 'Kidderminster's **quality** *football* lacked a *cutting edge* until the **introduction** of Williams in the 73rd minute'.

Cynical: Widely used of fouls (rather than of the player committing the foul) when the culprit knows exactly what he is doing. If the term **professional** *foul* risks dignifying such an infraction, the adjective *cynical* makes clear, within the parameters of restrained commentary, that it is unacceptable. The fact that an offence is **blatant** does not stop it from being *cynical* in intent, if not execution.

D

Danger: Shorthand, particularly in radio commentary, for a general attacking threat: 'The *danger* was *cleared* by Unsworth'. At *set pieces* the commentator is naturally keen to identify more specifically where the *danger* is likely to come from, whether it be from the *dead-ball **specialist*** himself or his intended targets: 'Mikhailovic is especially *dangerous* from these positions'; 'Dean Richards is coming up for this one and he's always *dangerous* from *set plays*'.

Date: 'Highbury *date* for Millers'. Cup ties which *capture the imagination* are often announced in this headline form by excited local journalists, who also claim that the *whole town* is ***buzzing*** with excitement. It would be possible, but less probable, to read 'Millmoor *date* for Gunners'.

Deadly: Used of a ***marksman*** whose aim is true within a certain yardage. Sometimes twelve: 'But Gray, usually *deadly* from the spot, hit a post with the penalty'. Sometimes inside six: 'it was a great cross in and we all know Quinn is absolutely *deadly* from that range'. Also reserved specifically for Doug Ellis because of his propensity to sack managers. Jimmy Greaves came up with the word when he saw the chairman clubbing a fish to death, but Mr Ellis felt sufficiently flattered to appropriate the epithet for the title of his autobiography, copies of which are still available in the club shop.

Deal with: On the pitch goalkeepers or defenders *deal with* difficult balls; off the pitch, clubs *deal with* problems *in the camp*. In the second case the voice is invariably passive: 'It's been *dealt with* internally and

I've no more to say on the matter while we're still in La Manga'. Despite there being no more to be said on the matter, it usually becomes ***well-documented***.

Debut: One of the many mysteries of football is the eternal importance attached to the identity of the opposition in your first match: 'Schmeichel, who is married with two children, made his United *debut* against Notts County'. Player profiles rarely fail to include such a seemingly incidental piece of information. But the noun *debut* (preferred to the less glamorous 'first appearance') conspires to make it seem important. Journalists who imagine genteel readers and don't work for a Eurosceptic editor have even been known to spell it *début*, complete with accent.

Deck: Synonymous with *pitch*, usually when the ball is being *pumped* in the air too much. 'Thistle should keep it *on the deck* more and *put their foot on the ball*'.

Deep: When a ***back four*** defends *too deep* (never 'deeply') the line it is holding invites the opposition to come onto them. Elsewhere on the pitch, players can take up a deliberately *withdrawn* position: 'Roy Bentley was a *deep-lying* striker before they were fashionable'. *Deep* is also used in a variant description of a late ***show***: 'Rochdale's equaliser came *deep* into ***stoppage*** *time*'.

Deflection: We can identify two sets of qualifiers to go with this. The first, for any *deflection* of more than a foot, consists almost exclusively of *wicked*. The second, for a barely noticeable deviation, comprises *slight, faint*, the *merest*, a *suspicion of*. Soi-disant neutral commentators tend to abhor *deflections* on behalf of the victimised team as *cruel*. Rarely are they welcomed as 'fortuitous' or 'lucky'.

Deny: Strikers seem to be more often *denied* by the *woodwork* or players on the line than by goalkeepers: 'Saunders rounded the keeper only to be *denied* by the angle of post and bar'. In such examples, the *woodwork* is felt to exert a malevolent influence of its own. From the keeper's perspective, such interventions are more welcome: 'Given saved from Henry with the help of a *kindly* upright'.

Derby: A *derby* match can be expected to prove *dour* in Yorkshire and *pulsating* everywhere else. The adjectives *typical* and *real* make the term *local derby* seem for a moment less tautologous. How local a *derby* has to be to qualify as such is becoming more elastic to judge by recent claims for Watford v Leeds (an *M1 derby*) or Niger v Chad (a *sub-Saharan derby*).

Diminutive: A long word for a short person. It is only ever used of players. Commentators will not speak of a 'diminutive stand' or a 'diminutive dog on the pitch'. Smaller *custodians* can be *diminutive*, but tend rather to be described as *not the tallest* of goalkeepers, while *pint-sized dribblers* have at least been bestowed with a *low centre of gravity*.

Director of football: More often than not, managers *kicked upstairs* and given this portentous title quickly learn that they are certainly not one of the club's directors, and that they will not be allowed by their successor to have anything to do with the football. At Southampton, a *performance director* has been watching from the wings.

Disappear: The pejorative verb used of flair players who *go missing* when the going gets tough. Football parlance naturally prefers the pleonastic version, as in: 'After they went one down, Joe Cole *completely disappeared* in the second half'. Compare *anonymous*.

Disappointed: 'He'll be *disappointed with that*' is
what commentators say when they mean 'that was
rubbish'. If this is not tentative enough, then add 'by
his own very high standards'.

Disputed: The classic term for a contentious decision, inviting or even insisting upon the adverb *hotly*.

Disrespect: Used disrespectfully: 'No *disrespect* to
Burnley, but we would expect to beat them over
two legs'. If a shock victory is obtained, Burnley will
then get *all **credit*** from the opposition manager, still
reluctant to believe he has been beaten.

Dissent: Remember that dissent is *shown* rather than
expressed. 'Poyet *showed dissent* to the officials' is
therefore orthodox, whereas 'Poyet dissented from the
officials' view' would be irregular.

Distribution: A ***service*** offered by goalkeepers when
throwing or kicking the ball to team-mates. As with
dissent, always used as a noun, never as a verb. Thus
'Digweed's *distribution* was poor', not 'Digweed distributed poorly'. It can refer both to a specific throw
('good *distribution* there from Shepherd') and to general throwing or kicking ability ('Bosnich's *distribution*
was never his strong point').

Dive: It is held to be self-evidently true that, unduly
susceptible to continental habits *creeping in* to the
English game, footballers *dive* much more than
before to *win* penalties and free kicks. There is now
even a FIFA-authorised technical term for the practice, which does not seem to have disconcerted the
worst offenders: 'Brian Barwick's brave pledge to
eradicate *simulation* looks about as convincing as an
El-Hadji Diouf *swan-dive*'. The word *dive* (to be used
whenever a player deliberately falls or tumbles, even

if it looks nothing like a *dive*) has become contami-
nated for other purposes. It is now sometimes
avoided when goalkeepers *throw themselves around*:
'Rustu *flung himself* to his left to *foil* Roque Junior'.
Indeed, *dives* by keepers now tend to be reported only
when they are *despairing*.

Dive in: *Diving in* looks no more like actual diving
than does much of the diving considered above. The
verb is used to describe any ill-judged, rash attempts
to win back the ball. 'Don't get me wrong, young
Titus is a good defender and he's *learning all the
time*, but he's got to stop *diving in*'. Defenders are
told to *stay on their feet*, rather than *go to ground* too
easily.

Dodgy: The terrace chant is *dodgy keeper*, and this
expression occasionally finds its way into press
reporting. You can also complain about *dodgy decisions*, or admit that recent results have been *a bit
dodgy*.

Domestic: An adjective now more in evidence
thanks to the marketing of the ***Champions League***.
Domestic form refers to recent results in your national
league, perhaps surprisingly away as well as home.
As in cycling, there is the understanding that *domestic* is unglamorous: 'After a dip in their *domestic form*,
Monaco will be looking forward to the visit of the
Italian champions'. Mind you, watching Liverpool
play Chelsea for the umpteenth time in some
academic group match makes us hanker for the good
old days.

Double save: A situation where a goalkeeper *can
only parry* the initial shot but stops the *rebound*.
Often coupled with *instinctive* or *incredible*, even
when the second save is fairly straightforward. But do

not say 'double shot'. If a striker gets two *stabs*, then it is more usual to talk of *two bites of the cherry*.

Doubt: Associated in pre-match speculation with injuries that may or may not **rule out** a player: 'Curran remains a major *doubt* ahead of Tuesday's showdown'. Similarly, 'Toshack and Heighway are definitely out, while Neal and Keegan are *doubtful*'. The underlying sense is that the physio looking at Neal and Keegan is *doubtful*.

Dream: Footballers *dream* exclusively about initiations. So whereas 'Alan Smith's goal at Anfield sealed a *dream debut*' or 'West Ham's Premiership season got off to a *dream start* with an early goal', the happy ending calls for another idiom: 'It was a *fairytale finish* for Le Tissier and Southampton at the Dell'. **Nightmares** are never premonitory in football.

Dressing room: A prosaic title for this location which hides a host of metonymic possibilities, since it often acts as the barometer of feelings in the camp: 'It was a sombre *dressing room* after Jones's injury, I can tell you'. A manager will sometimes wish that he had a *louder* dressing room or that it contained more **characters**. But too many *characters*, and he might *lose the dressing room*, the prelude to losing his job. Or again, a manager keen to emphasise a player's **contribution** beyond the verifiable attributes (goals, **assists** per season) may try to *appease* sceptical fans with this reasoning: 'Viv may have his best years behind him, but I know he will be a great addition to the *dressing room*'. The *boot room*, a step further into the mysterious recesses of a football club, will always be associated with Shankly's Anfield. Coaching *staff* at other clubs must content themselves with a *backroom*.

Dribbling: Seemingly less common these days, perhaps because too many clubshops sell bibs sporting the words 'I *dribble* for the Reds' (suitable for ages 0-3), or perhaps simply because *dribbling* is itself less common. Although schoolboy coaching manuals still feature sequential illustrations designed to 'improve your *dribbling* skills', the word seemed to go into semi-retirement on the day Stanley Matthews died. Now there seems to be a growing number of replacement verbs available, some of them perhaps spawned by journalists' holiday destinations: 'Rommedahl, buoyed by his goal, *slalomed* his way round the Newcastle defence'; 'Jay-Jay Okocha *shimmied* like a fish in a coral reef'.

Drift: Like **curl** or *float*, a verb describing the **measured** *delivery* of corners and free kicks: 'Simon Osborn *drifted* a free kick into the area'. Also used to describe the intermittent **disappearance** of flair players: 'The trouble with Leighton James is that he *drifts in and out* of games'. However, strikers can *go missing* in more effective ways: 'Sheringham *drifted off* his marker and headed beyond Walker'. It sounds for a moment as if Sheringham has fallen asleep when in fact he is a fully paid-up member of the *wide awake club*.

Drill: Used especially of low shots or low crosses into the box: 'After **good work** by Andy Welsh, Breen *drilled* into the net'; 'Nicky Forster outpaced the Town defence down the left before *drilling* in a *low cross* for Sidwell'.

Drop down: The reluctant action of many **elder statesmen** in order to *extend their careers* is to *drop down* a league or division.

Drop zone: Never 'drop area'. Somehow imported from wartime Special Overseas Forces operations, perhaps because teams in trouble are in need of reinforcements, but also linked to the idea of the **relegation** *trapdoor*. Teams in the *drop zone* look up dreamily to the *relative comfort* of *mid-table*. Interestingly, at the other end of the table there are *promotion places* and **play-off berths**, but no demarcated 'zone'.

Drought: Used either of teams that are *struggling in front of goal* or of strikers who cannot *buy a goal*: 'Steve McClaren spoke of his relief as his side finally ended their goal *drought* to book a place in the fourth round'. For extra effect, *droughts* should be measured in minutes: 'That's 3,455 minutes of football since Leaburn scored'. Conversely, on a lively afternoon, it can *rain goals*, but a *drought* is more often to be contrasted with a *glut* or *avalanche* of *goals* or, in recent parlance, a *goalfest*. *Famines* are less common, although you can talk of a striker's *lean spell*, while most fans will have experienced being *success-starved*.

Drubbing: 'Ipswich got their promotion chase back on track with a six-goal *drubbing* of *relegation-haunted* Nottingham Forest'. The Scottish prefer *gubbing*, which can apparently be used for any defeat of a frustrating or embarrassing nature: 'Mad TC had to be hauled away from the touchline by his chairman Mike Craig at the end of Saturday's 4–2 *gubbing* by the Lichties'. Terry Butcher has been in Scotland long enough to have learnt the vernacular: 'The day begins and ends in a "G" – a *gubbing*. We did not **turn up** today'.

Dubious goals panel: The FA's *Dubious Goals Panel* may look like a misnomer, in that it is supposed to verify retrospectively the identity of the goalscorer rather than certify the legality of the goal. But, then again, it will seem aptly named when in due course its adjudications prove baffling to players and fans who were at the game. Either way, it has given rise to a little commonplace in match reporting when different players may want to *claim* a goal, even at levels where any such panel is likely to be informal, as in this example from the Mid-Wales Youth League: 'The outcome is a matter for the *dubious goals panel*, Lewis appearing to get the **slightest of touches** on Fellows' *effort* before the ball ended up in the *empty net*'.

Dugout: The unglamorous quarters of the coaches and subs, sometimes (especially abroad) actually dug out of the ground, but rarely these days anything other than a perspex shelter. Like *dressing room*, used as a metonym for relevant personnel: 'The whole Werder *dugout* were up in arms about that decision'. **Nonsense** always gets more nonsensical if the *incident* which sparked it took place in front of the *dugouts*. At Villa Park, not to be confused with chants directed at the chairman. See **Deadly**.

Dumped: Verb used for a shock and/or humiliating *exit* from a cup competition: 'Stoke were *dumped* out of the cup by a *thunderbolt* from Frank Strandli'. Often combined with *unceremoniously*.

Duty: Noun always enlisted with the adjective *international*, usually to explain an absence from a club fixture and to transmit a sense that even money-grabbing footballers still obey a higher calling. For all the glamour and fame that it bestows on them, those who tread the *international stage* are essentially dutiful creatures, and indeed they *report for duty*.

Dynamo: Journalistic stand-by for the type of **all-action** player who powers his team forward in attack and plugs any gaps in defence. Recognised as a cliché by Eamon Dunphy in the 1970s – 'Les O'Neill's a real *human dynamo*, as they say in Fleet Street' – and still in use, even if not as many people cycle to football matches nowadays. See **midfield** for a range of such expressions.

E

Eager: As an adjective, commonly inflated to *ever-eager*, pertains to the willing **target man**, happy to receive the ball at all opportunities. In adverb form, used of **derbies** or games where leading teams have a chance to *renew* their rivalry: 'The return fixture between Watford and Leeds has been *eagerly anticipated* all along the M1'.

Early: Managers often insist on their sides *getting into* the other side *early*, without quite specifying how long this phase of the game will be. The Big-Ronism was *early doors*. Compare **first fifteen minutes**.

Earn: Whereas a single point in the league tends to be *salvaged*, a replay in the cup has to be *earned*. *Footballing* sides also need to *earn the right to play* by showing the same level of physical commitment as more robust but less skilful opponents.

Easier to score: Used with incredulity, and invariable past conditional and comparative forms: 'it *would have been easier* to score'. But when a player does score, commentators rarely say that it was indeed 'easy' to do so, nor do they remark when a difficult chance is taken that it was 'easier to miss'. See also **grandmother**.

Educated: A left foot can be *educated, cultured* or *trusty*. Right feet are never favoured in the same way. Are the owners of such left feet more thoughtful (Kevin Sheedy seemed intelligent, Liam Brady learned), or are the feet themselves somehow endowed with these attributes? You sense almost that the privileged limb has an identity of its own in the following spoken example: 'Hinchcliffe's got such a great left foot *on him* – if only he had a *yard* more of pace'. No-one seems to worry whether goalkeepers are left- or right-handed, probably because it does not matter, though it could be of more than *academic* interest to serious penalty-takers. See also *left-sided*.

Effort: Perhaps surprisingly, an *effort* can also be a goal: 'Notts County have pulled one back, another *effort* from McSwegan'. But more typically, when a goal fails to materialise, an *effort* will be described as *long-range* or *speculative*.

Elder statesman: Adopted euphemistically of an *old stager*: 'Stuart McCall's something of an *elder statesman* now but he still does a terrific job for us in the *engine room*'. Players who are in reality *past their best* can also be described as *evergreen* or *durable*.

Elect: Goalkeepers can be said to *elect to punch*, sometimes with the sub-text that democracy is not necessarily a good thing and that they should have tried to catch the ball.

Electric: Employed both of the *atmosphere* in a ground and the *pace* of players, so frequently that the adjective rarely has much charge.

Eleven: Football cares little for Roman numerals. The Duke of Arundel's XI is bound to be a cricket team. And whereas eights or fifteens or even sevens are common currency in rowing or rugby, *eleven* is used comparatively little in football as a collective number. But the motive is sharper when a team is unchanged: 'Ferguson is expected to name the *same starting eleven* for the second week in succession'. And there are two specific examples of motivational phraseology. A manager losing faith in most of his players can single out one of them: 'I wish I had *eleven Steve Claridges* in my team, I can tell you'. A manager asking his players to show him unlikely levels of *belief* will remind them that the other team's advantage is not numerical (at least until one of them gets sent off): 'Of course we're underdogs, but it's *eleven against eleven* out there'.

Elite group: Players join this when they pass a *milestone* for club or country: 'Owen joins an *elite group* of England players who have scored hat-tricks before the age of 21'. Sometimes the *elite group* created can be pretty contrived. It is not as if belonging to such a group confers any actual privileges, like an annual dinner, on the members.

Empty net: The *net* becomes *empty* only when the goalkeeper is no longer standing on his line in front of it. This ignores the fact that, even before keepers are *rounded* or *stranded*, the *net* itself is already empty (apart from that little kit bag thing many of them like to put in one corner).

Encounter: When a match is exciting it usually becomes an *encounter*, to be qualified further as *absorbing* and *fascinating* or *gripping* and *thrilling*.

Encroach: Has become the technical term for the specific circumstances in football when a player strays into the penalty area as a penalty is being taken, or a wall fails to keep ten yards away from a free kick. In the first instance it can be used absolutely with the specification of place understood: 'The ref wants it retaken. Someone must have *encroached*'.

End-to-end stuff: 'No goals, but this was English club football as the punters like it, *end to end*, cut and thrust, nip and tuck'. *End-to-end stuff* is a traditional cliché for a *flowing* or *pulsating* game, usually when *gaps start to appear* in defences or both attacks are looking lively. The more fashionable alternative in modern usage is to say that the game has become *stretched*. Summarisers are also fond of saying that there have been *chances at both ends*.

Energy levels: In the good old days it was about how fit you were, but since John Barnes started kicking isotonic sports drinks into waste-bins after ninety minutes of sheer hell, *energy levels* is the pseudo-sports science term.

Energy-sapping: Used of humid **conditions** or heavy pitches and reserved especially for the *turf* of **Wembley**.

Engine: 'Once a **box-to-box** midfielder with an *engine* that could have graced the 24 Hours of Le Mans, Roy Keane is now an influential, if injury-prone **presence** in the midfield'. Certain players are endowed with a great *engine*, the sum total of guts, *lungs* and heart. The *engine room,* more common in rowing to denote the middle numbers in an eight, can refer also to the midfield in football, particularly when players are getting *stuck in*. *Boiler room* is an alternative but seen, like steamships, less frequently nowadays.

Enough: When a defender does not effect a brilliant challenge but makes a sufficient nuisance of himself to nullify a *goal-threat*, he is said to have *done enough*.

Epic: Often used in fairly mock-epic contexts: 'The *plucky* Spartans' *epic* resistance was broken on 14 minutes'.

Epitomise: A verb beloved of summarisers cogitating on their man-of-the-match awards: 'That tackle absolutely *epitomises* McMahon's **contribution** today, Peter'. Conversely, a reporter who needs to paint a more negative picture will tend to use the verb *sum up*: 'A *woeful* shot – that just about *sums up* their day'.

Equally at home: A formula, which recurs in the team profiles found in match programmes, for a player able to play in several positions: 'Gallas is *equally at home* at right-back or at the heart of the defence'. It is sometimes difficult to corroborate the reliability of the claim.

Equipped: 'Early signs suggest newly promoted Leicester are *equipped* to survive at the top level'. This usage, frequent when describing **yo-yo** teams, seems to suggest that Leicester have enough kits and spare footballs to avoid relegation, but the equipment here is of course the playing personnel.

Errors: 'The first half was poor fare and was *littered with errors*'. Games which are not for the **purist** may be described as a *catalogue* or, with a nod to Shakespeare (not the midfielder **released** by Grimsby to Scunthorpe on 7.7.97), a *comedy of errors*. See also **unforced error**.

Erupt: Crowds or the grounds containing those crowds can *erupt*, usually to acclaim a goal of significance – one that *breaks the deadlock* or *seals a win* (though, in the former case, a ground more often *comes to life*). However, a bad refereeing decision will also cause a stadium to *erupt*: 'Leeds Road *erupted* after Hackett showed Philliskirk the red card'. Perhaps the metaphor may be more likely than it sounds. *The Sun* once 'measured' with a heavy-duty clapometer the noise of the crowd at Wembley during an England v Poland match, concluding that Les Ferdinand's goal caused a noise 'louder than Krakatoa'.

-esque: The suffix slapped, however awkwardly, onto a surname if an exploit recalls the **trademark** of a hero of yore: 'King's neat little **chip** from 40 yards out was almost Hoddle-*esque*'.

Everything: 'He made sure he took *everything* there, John'. In this context *everything* means *man and ball*, and it has been *taken* in the most uncompromising fashion. When a **hospital pass** leaves a player vulnerable to being **clattered** in this way, the tackler can be said to have a *free hit*.

Everywhere: 'Brian Flynn seems to be *everywhere* at the moment'. Used of players who are apparently involved at every turn. Broadsheet writers have been known to use *ubiquitous*, which means their subject will have covered *every blade of grass*. Whereas, if a player is not having such a good game, the ball tends to *follow him around*.

Examination: Contrary to the press coverage of exam results and of grade inflation, when football matches are described as *examinations* (do not abbreviate to 'exam') they are always very hard indeed: 'Wales came through the *sternest* of *examinations* against Italy and must go into the Serbia game with great heart'.

Example: Managers or players keen to pay tribute to the captain of the team will often state, impressively

if a little vaguely, that he *leads by example*. Captain
Marvel, Bryan Robson, the ***first name*** *on the team
sheet* (when he wasn't the first name on the ***treatment*** *list*) always *led by example*.

Exhibition: Usually combined with ***stuff*** to indicate
a situation where a team can ***afford*** to play in second
gear and indulge themselves with a few tricks: 'The
goal meant United could turn on the *exhibition stuff*
after the break'.

Exile: When players pre-emptively announce their
retirement from international football, they begin a
self-imposed exile. When managers are given a *touchline ban* they are *banished* to the stands. Both terms
are grandiose, given that usually the player continues
to *ply his* ***trade*** in his home country and the manager
gets to enjoy a better view of the game.

Expose: Encountered in the passive to indicate that
a player or defence have had their *limitations* or ***frailties*** *exposed*. Equally, players who do not ***track*** *back*
can leave their defensive colleagues *exposed* (whereas
good *holding* players *protect* them). In David Coleman
hyperbole, defences could be *stripped naked*.

Extra man: When the opposition has a man sent off,
the emphasis always falls on the *extra man* of the
other team, which acquires a mythical supernumerary player. The advantage can turn out to be a burden: 'West Ham, even with the *extra man*, could not
beat the keeper'. Not to be confused with the *spare
man*, who is the *libero* when a team plays a *sweeper
system* rather than a *flat* ***back four***.

Eye: 'Ballack *eyes* Premiership move'. Beloved of
Ceefax and tabloid headline-writers, the verb seems
especially suited to the initial manoeuvring before a

transfer, although players may also *eye* a comeback from injury or an international call-up. Whatever the context, the verb exempts the reporter from promising that anything will happen. When one player *makes eyes* at another, the situation is nothing more flirtatious than a striker looking to **send the keeper** the wrong way.

F

Facet: 'They outplayed us in *every facet* of the game'. Nobody seems to have elucidated what or exactly how many the *facets* of the game are but this is the phrase wheeled out, to include *each* or *every* such *facet*, when teams have taken a thorough beating. Alternatives are *every phase* and *every department*.

Factor: To every time there is a season, and to every football match there is a *factor*: *the injury factor, the time factor, the fear factor, the wind factor, the experience factor, the psychological factor, the unknown factor, the Ronaldo factor*. Like **situation** or **stuff**, a word that often pops up in commentary without meaning very much.

Fair play: On these islands we leave it to cads like Jonathan Aitken to take up the shield of British *fair play*. Only FIFA seems to take the concept of a *Fair Play Award* seriously. Indeed, in our football, it is rather embarrassing to win these awards, particularly if you *flirted with* relegation all the while. So you sometimes see references such as: 'Arsenal might not be winning any *Fair Play Awards* this season, but you have to say they are *durable* on the road'. Compare **sporting**.

Fair share of goals: 'Rocastle *weighs in* with his *fair share of goals* from midfield'. Unless they really have an *eye for goal* or, conversely, score so seldom that we are in the realm of ***collector's items***, midfielders tend to be assessed in these terms, whether in programme notes or pre-match analysis.

Fair-weather fan: Now that ***roofs*** cover most grounds in England, *fair-weather fan* is to be understood figuratively in the main as someone who turns up only when the going is good for his club. But we can imagine a time when *fair-weather fans* stayed away simply because they didn't want to get wet.

Faithful: Used in conjunction with the team name or, more commonly, that of the ground. It is broadly synonymous with *fans* but adds the implication that these fans are *long-suffering*, that faith is indeed required of them: 'The Edgar Street *faithful* saw United slip to another home defeat'. You can also refer to *die-hard fans* or the *hard core*, the latter phrase also hinting that this element may be *tasty* as well as *faithful*.

False position: 'Early days of course, and I think we'll find Southend are in a *false position*'. So this pundit thinks Southend have not been playing as well as their results *suggest* and, if he is really prepared to back himself against the truism that the *table never lies*, will duly promise to shave his head or run up Southend Pier in his birthday suit if he is proved wrong. His words are duly ***pinned up*** in the dressing room.

Fanatic: Noun for fans who really are fanatical: 'A real Derby *fanatic*, Toner flew in from Kuala Lumpur especially to see the Rams take on Mansfield in the Carling Cup'. This is because the truncated word *fan* has come (quite recently it seems) to mean a person present in the crowd rather than a supporter given to fanaticism. Similar deflation has occurred in Italian where the counterpart, *tifoso*, has become domesticated. Now *tifosi* just means *supporters*, rather than crazy fans who resemble victims of typhoid – the source of this term.

Fan-base: 'Cardiff have such a great *fan-base*, if only they could string together some results'. Clubs talk, like schools, about their *catchment area* (particularly when unfulfilled potential is being discussed), but it is more usual these days to talk of the *fan-base*, which seems to be something more active than a *catchment area* and more passive than the crowds a club gets, smaller in size than the former, but greater numerically than the latter. Perhaps it's the footballing counterpart to a political party's floating voters, or maybe certain clubs will always have to deal with a *fickle public*.

Fancy: 'I know that when Howard took over he didn't *fancy* Graeme as a player and he'd nearly sold him to Aberdeen'. This is the standard synonym for 'rate' in football. Managers would not take kindly to the word being interpreted in any other ways. Players can also be said not to *fancy* a particular assignment, perhaps if they have to play on a **bobbly** pitch in Volgograd in February up against a full back with the worst disciplinary record in the Russian league. Hence *fancy Dans* are viewed with the same suspicion as **big-time** *Charlies*, and certain players can develop a reputation: 'When Mark was younger there had been a feeling in the game that he was what was called a *non-fancier*. That meant that if you *rattled* him **early** he lost interest'. Meanwhile, entire teams can fail to be *up for* tricky games at **unfashionable** places, especially if John Beck has been putting too

much sugar in their tea: 'Cambridge were now playing some pretty big clubs, like Wolves, Derby and
Sunderland, who just didn't *fancy* it'.

Favours: For some reason, there is an assumption in
football that teams with *nothing left to play for* should
be courteous enough not to *dent* another side's ***aspirations***: 'Well, my old pal Sam Allardyce *did us no
favours today*'. During games, a bad pass does the
player attempting to control it – often the goalkeeper
– *no favours*: 'That backpass from Edwards did Dibble
no favours at all but he ***dealt with*** it'. Court intrigue
pre-dates football but *fall out of favour* is often the
phrase to describe the situation of a player who does
not *feature* in the manager's *plans* at present.

Feet: 'Glanford Park is *on its feet*. Beagrie, ***inevitably***,
has scored'. Pre-Taylor Report, a phrase which could
be used only at Highfield Road and Pittodrie, but an
increasingly popular way of announcing that a goal
has gone in at an all-seater stadium. Many reporters
will still prefer to tell you that the ground has ***erupted***.

Fifty-fifties: An economical way of describing the
situations in football where the ball is momentarily
available to either side. In practice, these act as the
barometer of a team's commitment, its hunger, its
desire: '"I'm ***disappointed*** with that", said Yorath
after the match, "they were winning all the *fifty-fifties*:
we didn't *want it* enough"'.

Final: An adjective used in two ways to complain
about an absence of finality. Summarisers can bemoan
the lack of a *final ball* (an alternative to ***killer ball***)
and the lack of ***quality*** in the *final third*.

Find: 'Sinnott *finds* Les Taylor who *finds* Worrall
Sterling'. Football can, in these circumstances, sound

like a rather poor game of hide-and-seek. The verb offers itself when you want a quicker alternative to 'passes it to', and is therefore most frequent in radio commentary, where speed is essential. But maybe the usage also suggests some *vision* on the part of the player *finding* his team-mate, while repeated use of the transitive verb, as in the above example, helps to evoke a *flowing move*.

Finish: Takes a variety of adjectives, in descending order of shot velocity: for those that *bulge* the *back of the net*, *emphatic*, *blistering* or *devastating* (these *finishes* also tend to be *rammed home*); for those that are placed, *assured*, *clinical*, *calm* (these tend to be *slotted home* or *passed in*); for mishit shots, *scruffy*, *scuffed*, *shinned*; for *efforts* that miss altogether, *not the best* of, *awful*. The noun *finisher* tends not to appear on its own as a synonym for *goalscorer*, but in a comparative or descriptive phrase: 'Romario is one of the best *finishers* in the world'.

Finished article: Used by managers to refer to *emerging youngsters* in their squads who are *not quite the finished article*. Once the necessary refinements have been made, they become *complete packages*.

Fired up: More common as an adjectival phrase – 'Tommy Docherty will have the *boys* all *fired up* for this one' – than as a verb: 'Tommy Docherty will be firing them up for this one'. *Up for it* is now perhaps as common: 'England are so *focussed* on their opening game on Tuesday that even Fred Street and Norman Medhurst are *up for it*'.

First action: In the era where substitute goalkeepers come on to face a penalty after the referee has applied a *strict interpretation* of the rules, this is the required phrase: 'Bennett's *first action* was to *pick* the ball *out* of the ***back of the net***'. But should the *first action* have been a save, use different terminology: 'Bennett made himself an *instant hero*'.

First fifteen minutes: The usual measure (although sometimes extended to *twenty* or even *twenty-five minutes*) for the *crucial first phase* of a match where the home team seeks to *come out of the traps* and the away side aims to *quieten the crowd* or *take the heat out* of the game: '*The first fifteen minutes* over there at the Olympic Stadium in Munich are going to be all-important'. A statement which proves false more often than not. See also ***early***.

First five yards: Distance used to illustrate the prowess of players who can *explode off the blocks* and have *pace to burn* over short distances. For slow older players, particularly Paul McGrath and Teddy Sheringham in recent times, the *first five yards* are *all in the head*.

First man: 'That's the third time in a row they've not got it past the *first man* at corners, Martin: you have to say that's poor'. It is close to a ***cardinal sin*** to hit the *first man* from a set piece crossed into the area, unless it is your own player ***flicking on***, in which case he is never described as the 'first man', even if he has *got in front* of his marker.

First name: Inspirational players can be described as the *first name on the team sheet*. When particularly attentive ***man-to-man*** marking occurs, you may say that the defender is getting on *first-name terms* with his victim.

First-team football: Very frequently combined with ***regular***, and the stated reason for most transfer moves by *fringe players*. There is also *nothing* like *first-team football* to hone a player's fitness, no matter how many reserve games he has *under his belt*.

First-time: As in *first-time* shot or cross. Appears most regularly in retrospect when a player has *squandered* the opportunity by taking an *extra touch*: 'He should have shot *first-time* instead of trying to *walk* it in'.

First touch: Ranges from *abysmal* to *exquisite*. Skilful players tend to have a *sure* or *assured first touch*. Another way of putting it is *instant control*. More prosaic talents tend to be *let down* by theirs. In crowd vernacular, particular objects of derision are chided for having the *first touch of a rapist*. Nor can they *trap a bag of cement*. For such players, the *second touch* is a tackle.

Fitness test: Almost invariably **late** (you never hear of a club booking in a player for a *test* at 2.30, four days before a match), and usually to be *undergone* by the **doubtful** player.

Flag-happy: Classic cliché for a linesman who does not give the attackers the *benefit of the doubt* in offside decisions. Similar formulations picture directors as *sack-happy* and referees as *card-* or *whistle-happy*, but the more usual adjectives in the latter case are *officious* and *fussy*.

Flattered: What polite footballers keen, very keen in fact, to move to a bigger club profess to be when one such comes calling. 'I'm *flattered* by United's *interest* (*obviously* may be added for further effect) but I remain on County's *books* at this moment in time'. This amounts to a **come-and-get-me-plea**. An *interest*, the inevitable prelude to an *approach*, can take different metaphorical forms, but courtship is the most recognisable one, as in: 'Cissé has already snubbed the *advances* of several European top clubs to move to Anfield'. *Flatter to deceive* is less common a phrase now, but may be used of teams that *huff and puff*, lack a *cutting edge* and are not quite the *sum of their parts*.

Flick-on: While a player can be described as *full of tricks and flicks*, a commentator will more naturally refer to a *flick-on* rather than just a flick, especially when a centre-forward backheads a long goal kick or someone like Steve Bould *gets a touch* on a near-post corner. The Big-Ronism for the latter case was *eyebrows*.

Floodlight failure: A rare occurrence these days but this remains the set phrase, never 'floodlight break-down', 'power failure', or 'blackout', always the alliterative *floodlight failure*. Floodlights may however be abbreviated to *lights* in such phrases as 'West Ham are brilliant *under the lights* at Upton Park'. *Big European nights* sometimes seem more exciting, perhaps because they trace their heritage to nights *under the lights* at Wolves in the 1950s. From a fan's perspective, when sighting the *glow of the lights* at an away ground of a certain vintage, you know you are no longer lost.

Flowing move: A *passage* of play where a team *strings together* some passes, often in an *exhibition* of *one-touch* football. *Flowing movement* can also be used, but *combination play* is now archaic.

Fly: To *let fly* is to shoot with force, usually from a specified distance: 'Lorimer *let fly* from 25 yards'. *Studs* may also *fly* in goalmouth scrambles of the *almighty* variety.

Follow: Footballers, unlike cricketers, do not 'follow on'. But they do *follow through*, when adding a foul to a tackle, or, more bluntly, *leaving their foot **in there***. They may also *follow up*, meaning *to score*: 'The Brentford keeper **spilled** the ball, and there was Nogan to *follow up*'. When the home **faithful** travel away they become a *following*: 'A tremendous *following* from Newcastle here in Barcelona …'. But those who say they *follow* a particular club rarely wish to mean that they *follow* the team on its travels. This implies a degree of detachment which distinguishes them from *fans*.

Football: An adjective for a little extra emphasis in a variety of contexts: 'We were taught a real *football lesson* out there today'; 'He has a first-class *football* brain'. Note also the gradation of meaning when *footballing* is used, suggesting **quality** but not necessarily fibre: 'There's no doubting they're a great *footballing* side'. The phrase *played all the football* indicates hyperbolically the superiority of one team over the other, often when this is not measured by the **scoreline**: 'City *played all the football* today but just couldn't *find* the **back of the net**'.

Football club: References to the *football club* are beloved of rabble-rousing managers or chairmen: 'He's Everton *Football Club* through and through'; 'No single player is bigger than this *football club*'. Announcements of great moment require the full title: 'Everyone at *Hull City Football Club* deplores the behaviour of this *tiny minority*'; '*Grimsby Town Football Club* have reviewed the clash between Justin Whittle and Alan Shearer. We feel that there was no deliberate *intent* on behalf of Justin to catch Alan with his arm'.

Footballistically: God loveth adverbs. Evidently, Arsène Wenger does too: 'I would like to celebrate this team, because they are really exceptional *mentally* as

well – not just *footballistically*'; 'We can do better
footballistically but the spirit is there'. This adverb
is common in Spanish and Italian but, to our knowledge, rare in French. When Graeme Souness or Alex
Ferguson starts using the term we will let you know,
although David Beckham can already vouch for the
latter's capacity to go foot ballistic.

Foray: When centre-halves enter the opposition half
in open play they tend to be described as *making a
foray*, whereas they just *come up* for *set pieces*.

Force his way: 'Jerome Thomas has *forced his way*
into the first-team reckoning'. While credit is given to
youth products for their inexorable progress through
the ranks, at the same time the obliging manager will
talk of *bringing* them *through*.

Foreign Legion: 'Next week Chelsea's *Foreign Legion*
comes to town'; 'It was the Magpies' *Foreign Legion*
that combined for the second goal'. The English language is still coming to terms with the growing prominence of overseas players in the game. This phrase
conveys both a sense of glamour and some suspicion
that these exotic stars are no more than a bunch of
mercenaries. Other such familiar, ready-made phrases
have been lifted, inappropriately, into football parlance to meet the new demands of describing foreign
contributions. Thus: 'Arsenal's *French connection*
set up the first goal'. Or: 'Forest's *Dutch Master* made
it 2-0'.

Form: *In the form of* is a staple construction when
reporting on football: 'Barnsley are *making a* **change**,
in the form of Dean Gorre'. Usually clumsy, often
redundant, it is to be found in some unsuspected
places: 'Plymouth have equalised, *in the form of* a goal
by Evans'.

Form book: Streets and gardens all over England must be littered with *form books* during the FA Cup, because we all know that the *form book goes out of the window* in that competition. When a cup-tie does *go to form*, the *form book* is never said to remain on the shelf.

Former: Very widespread usage to avoid renaming a player in the same breath: the *former* Albion stalwart, the *former* Spireites boss, the *former* Anfield favourite. See also **old boy**. If a player does not have a *former* club to provide commentators with a periphrasis, you may instead pay tribute either to his youth or to his loyalty: 'And now the Ulster *teenager* looks up…'; 'Brooking takes it on his chest and the *long-serving* Hammer **will** find Coppell…'.

Fortress: Preferred these days to the **cauldron** of old, *fortress* is to be used in tandem with the proper noun of the stadium, as though it were part of the address: 'Strasbourg, still without a point on their **travels**, have to visit *Fortress* Mestalla next'. Perhaps this is because, with **away goals** all-important in Europe, defensive records are at least as significant as intimidating **atmospheres**. However it is also possible for teams to man the walls in **domestic** competition: 'We have started to turn the Bescot into a *fortress* and long may it continue'.

Frailties: Tend overwhelmingly to be qualified as *defensive*, and are very often **exposed**. Attacks can be *toothless*, but never 'frail'.

Frame: References to the *frame* of the goal appear when it is *almost ripped from its moorings* by the *venom* of a shot. The *almost* is, in our experience, essential to the phrase. But there is a figurative use too, borrowed, it seems, from photography: 'Terry was not even *in the frame* there but somehow got back to make the **block**'. Here the defender had so much ground to make up that he had *no **right*** to effect a stop.

Free: When players are **completely** unmarked, they are often *gifted* a *free header*, although strangely never a 'free shot'. The phrase is used with admonishment when the header is duly missed: 'Chris Swailes had a *free header* there and should have done better'. *Free* as a noun is an abbreviation for *free transfer*: 'We picked him up in the summer *on a free* from Carlisle'.

Friendly: 'I always said the game against Argentina would not be a *normal friendly* but a *real* one'. The antithesis Sven-Goran Eriksson proposes here between *normal* and *real* seems unnatural but has been fostered in part by his own selection and substitution policies. Terry Butcher treated international *friendlies* as a 'private Agincourt' in his day, but the **stop-start** nature of contemporary non-competitive fixtures can render them *meaningless*. Unless, of course, the national team plays particularly badly or well: 'Far more *sparky* than the usual *"**after you, Claude**"* friendly with goals and *meaty* tackles swapped in the first 16 minutes, England's first match in Sub-Saharan Africa shimmered with *significance* far beyond 90 lucrative minutes' entertainment'.

Frustration: When a player on a team destined to lose commits an obvious foul, it ought not to be denounced as **cynical** but should be excused as an expression of *frustration* – whatever the circumstances. The noun is preferred to the participle, 'frustrated', and takes the adjective *sheer* or *pure*. 'Ouch, that was late, Mark – yes, *sheer frustration* from Ling there'.

Full cap: In order to distinguish international appearances at *senior level* from under-21 or youth team **honours**, it is usual to describe them as *full caps*. To anyone unversed in football parlance, the image of a half or *full cap* will seem odd. But in football circles these terms are now emptied of any literal, original meaning. Indeed, even though actual *caps* are still awarded, they can only really be spotted at auctions of football memorabilia or on the head of Paul Gascoigne when he **relaxes** at home. A *full appearance* distinguishes a player who starts from one who comes on as a substitute. But it does not mean, as you might suppose, that the player need complete the match. Some commentators, perhaps scrupulously aware of this, talk of 'Mutu's first *start* for Chelsea' rather than saying 'Mutu will make his first *full appearance* for the Blues'. See also **debut**.

Full force: Not as common as in boxing, but used especially when players in a wall are struck by a free kick flush in the face or another painful part of the **anatomy**: 'Murdo McLeod felt the *full force* of that one'.

Fully: An alternative to **all of**: 'Chevanton struck the free kick perfectly from *fully* 25 yards out'.

Fun: In *Athletics & Football* (1887), Montague Shearman observed that 'most footballers play for *the fun* and *the fun* alone'. The *demands* of the modern game have taken all the *fun* out of football, as well as the definite article away from *fun*. The phrase *fun and games* is always sardonic as elsewhere in life – 'there was the usual *fun and games* from the Uruguayans before the sending off' – and when strikers *bang them in for fun* or wingers *go past a man for fun*, this is a measure of effortlessness rather than enjoyment.

Furrow: The traditional **channel** in which the *lone striker* finds himself if his manager is playing only *one* *up*: 'Johnson continued to *plough* his usual *lonely furrow*'. In this kind of system the *front man* often has to live off **scraps**: 'Poor Darren Bent had to *forage* alone up front'.

G

Galactico: The *likes of* Puskas and Di Stefano were merely **legends**, whereas now Thomas Gravesen qualifies for *galactico* status. A term first eagerly embraced by English journalists: 'Lining up with the *galacticos* has added a new dimension to Beckham's play'. Then a standard way of not repeating the team's name in successive sentences: 'The faltering *galacticos* avoided the embarrassment of an early exit from the Champions League'. Soon used with irony in **domestic** reporting: 'When results go against Bolton, supporters speak of the club being a *galactico* retirement home'.

Gamble: Managers can *gamble with* an unusual tactical plan or *on* a player's fitness (sometimes the player himself can choose to *gamble*, perhaps with a *course of injections*, if the game is big enough). The main in-play usage occurs when a midfield player has to decide whether to *bomb on* into the **final** *third* after a potential **lost cause**, therefore making *defensive duties* more difficult if the move should break down: 'Lee Hendrie really should have *gambled* there and got himself *on the end* of Angel's **flick-on**'.

Game: Denotes both particular matches – 'Albion were never *in the game*' – and the métier, the profession: 'Robson has been *in the game* long enough to know that these are early days'. Older ex-professionals (particularly dear old veterans who don't realise how much present footballers earn) like to say 'the *game* has given me a great life'. Note also the phrase to denote a team or player given a ***torrid time***: 'Palace left-back Gary Borrowdale certainly knew he'd *been in a game*'.

Game, set and match: Football looks to other forms of recreation to express the definitive moment when a match is *all over as a* **contest**. Depending on whether you prefer tennis to playstation, you can use this traditional phrase or the equally remorseless but snappier *game over* as the way of indicating that there is no *way back* for the conceding team. *Curtains* can still be drawn on the proceedings, while the recondite options on offer might include *Goodnight Irene*, *Goodnight Nurse* and *Goodnight Vienna*. Of course, there are quite a lot of definitive moments that only might have been: 'You have to say, Rob, that if Russell had stuck that one in it *would* most definitely have been *game over*'.

Gaping: This term enhances the prospect of an ***empty net***, only to give more exposure to a *glaring* miss: 'Sibierski shot into the side netting with the goal *gaping*'. The transposition of terms in the next example can be read either as an adjustment which seeks to respect the convention or simply as unconventional: 'Rooney *tucked* the winner into a *glaringly empty net*'. We will leave the reader to decide what happened on this other occasion: 'Bryan Hughes was left with the goal *at his mercy*'.

Gasheads: Somebody in the *red half* of the city came up with this term of abuse owing to the location of Bristol Rovers' original ground. As so often, the term has been adopted and made safe by the fans abused: compare *Bluenoses, Gooners, Mackems, Monkey Hoyers,*

Scummers, Yids. On the other hand, as far as we are aware, Northampton Town called themselves *Cobblers* before anybody else did.

Gate: Less common these days to describe the attendance at a game (as in *average gate* or *gate receipts*), perhaps now that the size of the *gate* matters less than replica shirt revenues and TV rights, or because the modern turnstiles that clubs try to get fans through look less like *gates*.

Gel: Once a noun spread on the hair of footballers, now a verb which crops up at the beginning of the season as new players *bed in*: 'Once Chelsea's new superstars begin to *gel*, they'll be quite a team'.

Genuine: Failed attempts at gaining possession which result in a foul and are not to be classed as **cynical** should accordingly be categorised as *genuine attempts* for the ball.

Get a hand to it: When goalkeepers *get a hand to it* (*it* being the ball or shot), this phrase must always be followed by the conjunction *but*: 'Digby *got a hand to it, but* couldn't stop Durie from adding to his *tally*'.

Get hold: When a shot *travels*, it is customary to say 'he really *got hold* of that one'. Equally, if an **effort on goal** is **scuffed**, you can say 'he didn't *get hold* of that at all'. It is understood that getting hold of the ball does not mean *handling* it.

Get it right: 'Gerry Taggart had to *get that one right*, and didn't he just?' Since tackling in the penalty area leaves no margin for error, the words *get it right* are often uttered admiringly by commentators as they look at a crucial **intervention** or *last-ditch* tackle on the action replay. Never said of challenges elsewhere

on the pitch (unless the tackler is *on a yellow*). Nor
would you ever say 'he didn't get that right'.

Get out of jail: The phrase used almost automati-
cally by a manager whose side has been allowed a
narrow escape or given a reprieve by a superior team
on the day. Paul Sturrock acknowledges the cliché by
noting its origin: 'In *Monopoly* terms, we used our *Get
Out of Jail Free* card'. But the phrase only begins to
shed its formulaic quality when taken over by the
sports journalist: 'It was *get-out-of-jail* day for
Everton but the **new-look** Southampton will feel they
can also find an *escape route*'. Here the reporter has
concluded his piece by linking the idea of *jail* with
that of the **relegation** *trapdoor*.

Ghost: The more categorical word for a player who
flits in at the near post or *materialises* at the *back
stick* to score unopposed because the defence has
failed to detect the apparition: 'Owen *ghosted* in
unnoticed'; 'Crespo *ghosted* unseen into the action'.
Even the greatest defenders never seem able to lay
their hands on a *ghost* until the time comes to write
their autobiography (subtitled *My Story So Far* if they
are still playing).

Gift-wrapped: Commentators at work over Christmas often resort to metaphors involving gifts or
gift-wrapped chances when it comes to describing
defensive lapses: 'Colin Stewart *fluffed* an **improvised
clearance** and Derek Lilley was on hand to accept the
early Christmas gift'. In the same vein, a good goalkeeper who keeps *a **clean sheet*** during the holiday
period will encourage allusions to Dickens: 'Nicky
Johns, a veritable *Scrooge* for the Addicks, didn't let
anything by him'. It is always enjoyable to read match
reports in late December and find more inventive variations on a theme: 'Appropriately for the *pantomime*

pitch at East End Park it was a *man in tights*, Stilian
Petrov, who stole the show'; 'Mellberg needlessly
sparked more **handbag**-*wielding* than at the first day
of the *Christmas sales*'. But note *Christmas trees* can
be seen all the year round in football, as they are a
formation not a decoration.

Gilt-edged: Describes a good chance (usually missed)
either in front of goal or in a title race: 'Heaney missed
a couple of *gilt-edged* chances'; 'It was a *gilt-edged*
opportunity to go top'. To fluff a *gilt-edged chance*
may seem less costly than to waste a *golden one*, but
the two terms are used pretty much interchange-
ably. A variant usage may have been suggested by the
bling on show at White Hart Lane: 'Kanouté's cross
was a *gold-embossed **invitation*** to strike Tottenham
ahead'.

Give and go: *Touch and go* is heard in the treatment
room, *Wash and Go* seen in the dressing room, *give
and go* admired on the pitch. The busy staccato phrase
describes a particular action, a sort of **one-two** without the two, while the phrase *pass and move* refers to
a team given to such actions: 'Under McGhee, they
were a really good *pass and move* team, but now
they're just **Route One merchants**'. *Kick and rush*
was before our time, as was *push and run*.

Gleefully: 'Bakayoko pounced on the mistake and
gleefully slotted home'. The adverb is a little misleading here in that the *glee* tends to come after the
goal. Rarely do you see strikers beaming as they hit
the ball, like a cyclist raising his arms in triumph
before he crosses the line. Similarly goalkeepers are
described as *despairing* when they dive for a shot that
beats them, even though there are not normally signs
of outward despair (at least until the ball has hit the
back of the net).

Glorious: Oddly enough, used chiefly of chances or opportunities when they are not taken: 'It was a *glorious* chance to break the deadlock, but Agana *spooned it*'.

Gloss: When a winning team has suffered some setback, usually an injury, a sending off or a yellow card which earns a suspension, this is the required term: 'Vieira's **rush of blood** *took the gloss off* Arsenal's victory'. It is usual, furthermore, to add regretfully at the end of the report: 'but tomorrow's headlines will be *all about* Vieira'. For similar but more serious circumstances, when the *gloss* comes off comprehensively, see also **mar**.

Go down: *Going down* is perhaps the most common way of saying 'being relegated'. It is certainly the most common way of singing it (in the direction of the troubled club's *long-suffering* fans). In commentary, 'it *goes down* as a chance' and 'that has to *go down* as a miss' are frequent locutions. The verb is perhaps supposed to confer an official status on the chance or miss in question. A diving player is said to *go down* too easily.

Goal of the season: Brilliant goals are described, particularly during live commentary, in this way: 'What a *strike*! That has to be a *contender for goal of the season*'. *Contender* is often preceded by *early*, even when the season is far progressed.

Goalhanging: Gerund reserved for the behaviour on those schoolyards where the offside laws have no jurisdiction. Like *ballhogging*, never used in the professional game without irony.

Goalscorer's goal: The sort of goal *goalscorers* score – by inference, an unspectacular one. The tautology may be tautologised yet further by adding the adjective *real*: 'Lineker has **poached** another. This one was a *real goalscorer's goal*'.

Goalscoring opportunity: Since the change in laws, always takes *clear* in situations where players *deny* such an *opportunity* illegally, therefore incurring a **straight** red.

Go down the other end: Teams never seem to *go down the other end* to do anything apart from *score*. Used in particular to denote a quick riposte to a goal: 'After letting in a **soft** second, Argyle *went straight down the other end* to score through Chadwick'. When fans *go down the other end*, we have *disgraceful*, and nowadays very rare, **scenes** on our hands.

Good time to score: Traditionally, on the **stroke of half-time**. Yet, as pundits often duly confirm, it's not as if there is *a bad time to score*. The supplementary remark suggests that a *good time to score* is now one of those phrases which are stored in a mental box labelled 'to be used self-consciously'.

Good work: These words may praise an adroit piece of defensive play but more commonly describe penetrative running in the **build-up** to a goal: 'Arveladze *bagged* the second after *good work* by Fernando Ricksen'.

Got down well: What tall keepers have done when making a save. This is spelt out further in such constructions as *'he got down well* for *such a big man'*. *To his left* or *to his right* can be added to provide extra information for radio listeners.

Got good distance: In any situation where a keeper **elects** *to punch* and the outcome is successful, this tends to be the set phrase. We have never heard a commentator describe a goalkeeper's *kicking* in this way.

Grab: Sounds dramatic, at the very least stealthy, but sometimes used in a fairly neutral narrative way: 'The striker *grabbed* his second goal in stylish fashion just before the break'. But see **smash-and-grab raid**.

Grace: Nice verb employed almost exclusively in the past tense, usually with a hint of nostalgia: 'Redfern Froggatt, who *graced* Hillsborough for so many years, …'. Footballers so described must have been able, *in their pomp*, to **play a bit**. They are more likely to be *legends* than *loyal servants*, two of the nouns available in football parlance when assessing a past player.

Grandmother: Commentators and summarisers will often tease one another when indicating just how profligate a miss was – 'Even you could have *stuck* that one *away*, Alan' – but there are misses of such magnitude that *grandmother* needs to be wheeled in: 'Gary will be *so* **disappointed** with that miss – I think my *grandmother* could have knocked that in *with her eyes shut*'.

Grey hairs: When managers are not visibly pulling their hair out, you may nevertheless resort to saying: 'That piece of defending will give Ian Branfoot *a few more grey hairs*'.

Grind out: How you achieve a result by *ugly* methods: 'Coventry City survived the first-half dismissal of Bennett to *grind out* a precious point'.

Groundshare: A notion alien to the British psyche, stranger than sharing your wife with another man (especially if he supports the same team as you). Hence any proposal for a *groundshare* by a commercially minded chairman will not exactly *appease the fans*. Although you could talk about 'sharing a ground', the compound form in which noun and verb cling together in one word, *groundsharing*, is preferred, perhaps making the idea seem more particular and perverse.

Group of Death: A regular visitor to the language of football, this nice piece of hyperbole appears whenever World Cup draws are held, but can make an intermediate appearance at European Championships or other regional tournaments too. It is so familiar that commentators promptly debate which of the groups drawn might be *the Group of Death* this time round, as though it were a title which has to be assigned to one of them: 'Cameroon, Egypt, the Ivory Coast, Libya, Sudan and Benin – Group Three certainly looks *the Group of Death* in the African Zonal Qualifying'.

Guilty: 'Gillingham were *guilty* of profligacy in front of goal for much of last season'; 'After being *guilty* of missing two *gilt-edged* chances in the first half, Webber *atoned* with a superb strike'. *Guilt* never attaches to those who cheat, spit, maim or generally misbehave, but in football parlance it is instead attributed to a player who will merely be *disappointed*. As elsewhere in the game (see *cardinal sins*), the language becomes more moralistic as the infraction becomes less immoral.

Gulf: The noun employed invariably for a wide discrepancy in *class* or resources: 'The *gulf in class* between the two sides was all too evident *early doors*'; 'For Norwich the *gulf* in finance is simply too wide'.

Gutted: Such a familiar reaction from managers under the cosh that a degree of circumspection obtains about acknowledging it. Thus, 'Bryan Robson wore a sombre look that had *"gutted"* written all over it', while 'Sam Allardyce, always quotable, said he was "slightly *gutted*" '.

H

Had: Out of work managers, enjoying *a well-deserved rest* from football, often seem to find themselves acting as summarisers nevertheless. Their testimonies on behalf of particular players will exhibit a proprietorial form of nostalgia: '*I had* him at Birmingham, and he always showed great potential'; '*I had* Claudio *with me* at Sunderland, and his attitude is first-rate'. Sometimes, especially when Trevor Francis is speaking, the first part of the sentence is designed to explain its second part. Where a team *had* the ball in the net it will only have been in circumstances which caused the goal to be disallowed: 'Two minutes later Watford *had* the ball in the net through Marlon King, but the on-loan Forest forward was *adjudged* to have handled'.

Hairdryer: The legendary *treatment* conducted by Sir Alex Ferguson. The allusions continue to fly about in reports on his team: 'At half-time United traipsed down the tunnel for what was sure to be a fearful bit of *blow-drying* from their manager'; 'Ferguson was on his feet and fixing a glare in the direction of Kleberson – the *hairdryer treatment* from 70 yards'.

Half-time: Provokes alternative visions of the *half-time cup of tea* or the *half-time oranges*. Teams who have *let themselves down* in the first period usually have *lots to discuss* and do this *over* their chosen refreshment (see **teacups**). If the camera focuses on a manager whose side find themselves behind just before the *break*, he will usually be described as *pondering* his *half-time team-talk*. While a *game of two halves* is one of the oldest clichés in the lexicon, it is remarkable how often a team who has played very well or badly in the first period come out a completely *different side* after the break. Note also the increasingly prevalent habit of managers involved in *two-legged* **affairs** to think of the end of the first game as *half-time*: 'We did ever so well over there, but it's only *half-time in the tie* and I'll be warning my players against complacency'.

Handbags: Describes a contretemps in which *arms are raised* but which is not a full-blown fist-fight. The more *de luxe* versions are *handbags at ten paces* or *handbags at dawn*. But note a variant usage from Chris Coleman which does make *handbags* a synonym for real rough stuff: 'We don't want to see a 15- or 16-man mass **brawl** with *handbags* flying everywhere'.

Handful: Pertains in particular to centre-forwards who are physically imposing or difficult to **deal with** *pace-wise*. Sometimes coupled with *prove*: 'Dave Kitson was *proving* a real *handful* for the Orient defence'.

Handle: The way managers or maturing players *handle the pressure* or more particularly *handle the press* is *part and parcel* of the modern game. *Handling* can also be used in a similar context to indicate whether a wayward talent needs strong or sympathetic treatment, although the gerund is more commonly used of goalkeepers whose *handling* tends to be *safe* or *sure* if they are being praised, **dodgy** or *suspect* if criticised.

Hang up: 'I'm not quite ready to *hang my boots up* yet. I know I can still do *a* **job** at *this* **level**'.

Apparently, *hanging up their boots* is the action of footballers when they retire from the game. We suspect that most of them actually throw their boots away or put them in a cupboard if they cannot auction them off, but the image still thrives, just as most of us still *hang up* when we put the telephone down.

Hardest thing in football: As managers agree, this is not achieving back-to-back doubles, but telling a young apprentice that he will not make the grade and that you are *releasing* him. Should he come good later at another club, the proprietorial usage is still permitted, even on the day he might *come back to haunt you*: 'I *had* Peter at Coventry and had to let him *move on*: I'm so pleased to see him doing well for today's visitors'.

Hard man: Teams or countries only seem to be allowed one such *dirty* player: 'Ivanov is **many people's** idea of the *hard man* of Bulgarian football'. *Hard-tackling* also means *dirty*.

Has: 'Ronnie *has seen* Kevin McDonald making a smashing run down the right. *Kev's* hit a terrific cross and *I've* taken it down on my chest and *I've* just had a crack at it really'. When footballers *talk us through* a goal they've scored, the perfect tense is often preferred to a more conventional past historic. Such descriptions gain in immediacy what they might lose in accuracy.

Hatful: While a **hat-trick** is definitely three scored – enough to take home the **matchball** – a *hatful* tends to stand for the unquantified number of chances that go begging: 'Marlon Harewood *spurned* a *hatful* of late chances'; 'Crouch *squandered* another *hatful* against Betis in midweek'. However, *hatfuls*, like *pots*, can be units of measure for a goal tally counted over a season or career: 'With his shirtcuffs in his fist, Denis-Law style, Biley was *banging in* the goals by the *hatful*'.

Haul: Another collective noun for *goals* in the context of a game or a season.

Head: If *heads go down*, so too will the team to which the heads belong. *Heads up*, on the football pitch, is not the result of the opening toss but what players say to each other when they have conceded a goal. If you are Graham Taylor, it's also the time for *chin up and chest out*. *Head tennis* denotes a **passage** *of play* when the ball passes back and forth in the air between teams. There seems to be no equivalently neat expression when this happens on the **deck**, although *human pinball* is a seldom-seen candidate.

Header: A selection of adjectives is available to reporters. For power: *crashing, resounding, thumping, unstoppable*. For trajectory: *angled, downward, glancing, looping*. For height (of the man heading the ball not the ball itself): *imperious, majestic, towering*. For control: *crisp, cushioned, well-directed*. For the lot: **bullet**. If a player is *good in the air*, say that he is an *excellent header of the ball* rather than just 'excellent at heading'.

Hearts: 'Stags' hearts broken by late Lua Lua *leveller*'. *Hearts* are always broken in football by decisive late goals, and not, as you might imagine, by a crushing defeat or by a sickening injury (when you would use **mar**). Usage in Scotland is of course conditioned by the presence there of a team popularly known as *Hearts*.

Heavy: When an injury is taped up, the strapping applied always seems to be *heavy*. Similarly, **doubtful** players always seem to have a *heavy* cold or bout of flu to distinguish them from less resilient souls who cry off work. Meanwhile, Joe Royle has had such a raw deal from referees that he seems to have defined a new ***bookable offence***: 'We've had penalties given against us this season for *heavy breathing*'.

Helpless: Managers and goalkeepers in particular turn out to be *helpless*. The former *look on helplessly* from *the sidelines* as their team loses. The latter are ***exposed*** by defensive shortcomings: 'Shilton was *left helpless*, as the ball trickled past him'. Here *helpless* means both 'powerless' and, to an extent, 'blameless'. The adjective generally exonerates the keeper, but, to make sure, you may add 'Shilton could do *nothing* about that one'.

Heroics: Can be used of a fine individual performance in adversity but more commonly reserved for the achievements of ***unfashionable*** managers and clubs: 'Dario Gradi has performed absolute *heroics* in keeping Crewe in Division One for so many seasons'. A variant is *minor miracle*.

High-flying: The adjective discreetly lends itself to describing a club unaccustomed to the upper echelons of its division. This club may indeed find itself, like Icarus, in a ***false position***: '*High-flying* Huddersfield travel to Chelsea in the next round'.

High line: 'Once again Rangers are flirting with disaster playing such a *high line* against a player of Clinton Morrison's pace'. This term refers to a defence *pushing* right *up* towards the halfway line in an attempt to *squeeze* the play, with a likelier risk that the *offside trap* will be *sprung*. From the technical point of view, the converse of *defending too **deep*** – and just as suspect.

High-profile: Interchangeable with *big-name*. Adjective describing certain *larger-than-life* managers, and the kind of transfer deals they transact, which do not necessitate **wheeling and dealing**. A word so popular with journalists that it can even be employed for *glaring* errors on the pitch: 'Carroll's *high-profile blunder* leaves United with a **mountain to climb**'.

History: Some commentators would have you believe that *history* really began when the **Premiership** was founded: 'Colin Cameron headed the winner and made Wolves *history* with their first *Premiership* goal'. Others go back to the Second World War as the starting point, considering the nineteenth-century exploits of teams like Surrey Rifles and Bon Accord, with their big scores and big shorts, to be anomalous and distorting. All clubs have their own proud *history* in the form of **annals**. But should there be *some history between* two clubs or two players, it is a euphemistic way of referring to previous *bad blood*, invariably of recent date.

Hit and hope: Perhaps more apposite for snooker players faced with a difficult escape shot or golfers playing from an impossible lie, but also used in football either of individual strikes (even more **speculative** than when one is **shooting on sight**) or styles of play: 'It's all *hit-and-hope* **stuff** from Bournemouth now in these final minutes'.

Hit back: When teams score a quick equaliser, causing **celebrations** to be *short-lived*, they are often said to have '*hit back* almost immediately'.

Hobbit team: Football has always been *a physical game* and, in its modern form, those lacking in inches find themselves increasingly at a disadvantage. Perhaps *hobbit* will assert itself as the collective term for **pint-sized** or **diminutive**: 'When you look at the

size of Bolton and Everton, you'll get **murdered** if
you line up a *hobbit team* against them'.

Hold his hands up: Very popular cliché for a player
or manager acknowledging his error: 'Des Walker
will be the first to *hold his hands up* and admit it was
a **howler**'; 'Kelvin Davis has *held his hands up* for *letting in* the second'. Sometimes the player does indeed
hold up one or two hands immediately afterwards,
although the former can also be a gesture to claim offside and the latter a way of suggesting to the officials
that no **contact** has occurred.

Holiday on ice: A felicitous Keeganism to describe
an **almighty** *scramble* where players slip or slide: 'I
don't know what Ravelli was playing at, Brian, but it
was *holiday on ice* **stuff** out there'.

Home: A magical word in the English language dear
to its speakers. It is cherished no less by football fans
and players, particularly those of Plymouth Argyle
for whom *home* is Home Park. *Home soil* or *home
advantage* are prized more than on the continent
where clubs will **groundshare** with their bitterest
rivals. Before cup draws you will often hear said: 'We
don't care who we play, as long as it is a *home* tie'.

Homer: A referee whose decisions are perceived
to favour the home side: 'The Panathanaikos game
brought a whole new meaning to the word "*homer*"'.
Seldom heard because this sort of vocabulary (perhaps adapted from baseball) is neither vituperative
enough for most football fans nor temperate enough
for most football reporters.

Honours: *Honours*, to be found proudly listed on the
first page of a club programme, bracket the cups and
trophies, promotions and record victories that the

club likes to recall. Even in this age of ***ambition***, early-season reports can suggest a team has the ability to *challenge seriously for honours*. Should a match end with *honours even*, it's a draw, though a draw likely to be less boring than a ***stalemate***. *International honours* is the standard heading on your *CV* if you can boast of appearances for your country.

Hook: 'The *gaffer* gave me *the hook* at half time, and I was obviously not happy'. The *hook* is a trade term merely for being *pulled off* rather than being punched in the face, however irate your manager. Meanwhile, players seem to *hook* the ball only when they are clearing it *off the line* or *away* from danger: 'Although Roy was ***stranded***, Livi midfielder Allan Walker was handily placed behind him to *hook clear*'.

Hooligan: Originally, when people could still remember those Irish troublemakers, the Hoolickins, the term *hooligan* had nothing whatsoever to do with football. Then *football hooliganism* and *football hooligans* came to be. Now the term *hooligan* stands once again on its own, without need of qualification, but for the opposite reason that football is so utterly absorbed by the term. There may be something like fascination among those who talk about *hooliganism*, just as a term like 'road rage' may legitimate what others would call bad manners. But most people prefer the euphemistic *crowd trouble* when *disgraceful **scenes*** actually occur. Notice also that *hooligans* always are a *tiny minority*, even when there seem to be hundreds of them throwing seats across Kenilworth Road.

Hoops: Clubs more commonly wear stripes than *hoops*. An effect of this is that the few teams wearing *hoops* (Celtic, Morton, QPR, Reading) will, whether they like it or not, be called *the Hoops*. But never call a team wearing stripes 'the Stripes'.

Horse race: There are never more than two or possibly three horses in a race when, metaphorically, they represent championship or promotion contenders: 'It is only December, but it already looks like a *two-horse race*'. The metaphor can be extended if the contest goes *right down to the wire*. Remember also that the race is *a marathon not a sprint*.

Hospital pass: Such a common cliché for a bad ball that it sometimes gets abbreviated: 'That was *hospital* from Scimeca there'.

Hot seat: May be used to place particular emphasis on the pressures of management, but more commonly just a thesaurus version of *job*. Above all found in conjunction with the name of the ground: 'Houllier had been in the Anfield *hot seat* for too long'.

Hotbed: *The* football *hotbed* in England is the North East. You are allowed to call Merseyside and maybe Glasgow too *a hotbed*.

Howler: A glaring, perhaps amusing blunder, usually the province of the **schoolboy** (schoolgirls appear not to be guilty of *howlers*), as in 'the Equator is a menagerie lion running round the earth', but known also to occur on the football pitch. The discourse of commentary is a sustained attempt at disguising partisan views, but this term barely conceals some derision, maybe even a little *Schadenfreude*, just as others, like *agony*, betray some sympathy or frustration.

Huff and puff: 'Alex were content to soak up the pressure as their hosts *huffed and puffed*'. This expression indicates energetic but always ineffectual play. Kevin Keegan, in making the following remark, glances back to the origin of the phrase: 'We *huffed and puffed* but we never looked like getting the second goal that would have blown West Brom's house down'. The examples suggest that *huffing and puffing* is characteristic of the home side, as if they were trying, with increasing desperation, to demolish any *stall* that the visitors may have erected. Managers of the Glenn Hoddle school urge their teams to keep *playing football* and like to regard the breathless as the brainless: 'To come back like we did, it wasn't *huff and puff*, it was *cultured*'.

Hug: *Old-fashioned* wingers are sometimes encouraged to *hug* the touchline in order to afford their teams proper *width*: 'McManaman should be *hugging* the touchline, Barry, and not *cutting inside*'. Another way of putting it is *getting paint on your boots*.

I

Ill-tempered: The traditional adjective, for some reason preferred to 'bad-tempered' and combined with *affair* or *clash*, to describe a game where *handbags* have occurred or are likely to occur.

Immense: There are informal rules in football for the adjectives expressing unbounded enthusiasm. Use *immense* for an individual player or performance: 'Abdoulaye Faye was absolutely *immense* for us today'. Use *massive* for an *occasion*, a *result*, a *task* or a team you want to join: '*No disrespect* to Millwall, but Coventry are a *massive* club'. Use neither if you are overwhelmed by the magnitude of events: 'Bacup Borough boss Brent Peters said: "It is the *biggest* signing of my football career because they do not come any *bigger* than David May" '.

Impact: Typically used to convey a negative experience, and especially to describe an abortive, unhappy foreign sojourn: 'Blissett failed to *make an impact* in Milan'. *Impact player*, often with the additional phrase *from off the bench*, is borrowed from rugby as a modern alternative to the alliterative **super-sub**.

Improvised a clearance: Used when the keeper is out of his area and has to head or kick the ball to safety. Such *clearances* are invariably *improvised* or *unorthodox*, despite being the only legal alternatives available. Acknowledged as *effective* if successful; otherwise condemned as a **rush of blood**.

Incident: Exciting **encounters** are invariably described as being *full of incident* (the singular is always preferred to the plural in this phrase). Usually there is one particular *incident* to which one of the managers feigns momentary inattention: 'I must say I didn't see the *incident* involving *the **lad*** Richardson'. Such *incidents* become **talking points** back in the studio.

Indicate: This is the obligatory verb, to be used with due solemnity, when the fourth **official** shows how much time is to be added on: 'Jeff Winter has *indicated* there will be an additional three minutes'.

Industry: **Work-rate** may have rather superseded this term but it is still used to describe the efforts of players, especially in the **engine** room. If a midfield is *full of industry* there may be at least a suspicion that it is lacking in **quality**. The same inference sometimes comes across when a manager praises his players for *honest endeavour*: 'Stan Ternant hailed his side's "*endeavour* and *commitment*" – in other words, it was a rotten game'. However, the word *manufacture* is used narratively without any aspersions: 'Stewart

Petrie and Owen Coyle combined to *manufacture* a chance for Andy Smith'.

Inevitably: Employed in commentary, perhaps *inevitably*, when a *prolific* striker strikes: 'Phillips, *inevitably*'; 'Larsson, *inevitably*'; 'Clive Allen, *inevitably*'. During the 1994 World Cup, one commentator described Hagi as 'that *inevitable* man'. Also used, tipping your hat to Providence, when a player scores against his former club: 'Tebily, *inevitably*, popped up to score against the Blades'. It is a way of saying 'wouldn't you know it?', suggesting something more predestined than 'unavoidably'. There is also such a thing as an *air of inevitability* about a late goal conceded by a team that has not *put away* its chances.

Injury: Nobody (with the possible exception of Roy Keane) likes to see a player *injured*. But there are different gradations by which sympathy may be apportioned when injuries occur. If, say, 'Ferguson is *crocked*', this hardly compassionate way of putting it is likely to be that of rival, or at least indifferent supporters. When 'Big Dunc hands in another *sicknote*', this may be said by exasperated fans of his own team. Then there is a whole variety of phrases in which sympathy mixes with a bit of impatience: 'More injury *woe* for Duncan Ferguson', '*injury-prone* Duncan Ferguson', '*hapless* Duncan Ferguson, *dogged* by injuries', 'Duncan Ferguson has been *stricken* with another injury'; '*Ill-starred* Duncan Ferguson has had another injury *setback*'. Injuries sometimes *rule* a player *out*. The convention these days is to itemise team injuries in brackets after the name: 'Alexandersson (hamstring), Ferguson (knee, groin, ankle)'. Whole clubs can be *plagued* by injuries as though they were contagious.

Injury time: As opposed to *normal* or *proper* time. Since the advent of the fourth official's indicator, *injury*, *added* or **stoppage** *time* is often replaced, for greater specificity also, by references such as 'we are playing the second of the four *additional minutes*'.

Injustice: Commentators tend to use this as a reflection on what might have happened – 'it would have been an *injustice* had City equalised' – but it would be unexpected as an outright comment on what did happen. *Travesty* may also be used in the same context.

Innocuous: Qualifies **challenges** (rather than **tackles**) which seem *lightweight* but cause serious injury: 'It looked an *innocuous* challenge but I'm afraid Big Duncan now has a **problem**'.

Inside: 'Scotland, needing the win, were a goal down *inside* ten minutes'. This usage, apparently particular to football, is favoured when things happen quickly (ten minutes often being the measure, it seems) and indeed '*inside* ten minutes' maybe sounds quicker than 'after nine minutes'. It can therefore serve quietly sardonic purposes, as in the example above.

Instinct: Whereas some coaches get a reputation for being *defensive-minded*, others have *attacking instincts* which have to be tempered. This is one example of the way attackers, with their **poachers'** *instincts*, are distinguished from defenders.

Instrumental: Common way of recognising an individual **contribution** in a game or over a period of time: 'Kevin's been *instrumental* in our success this season'. The close cousin is *orchestrate*: 'Benarbia was *orchestrating* all that was good about City's play'.

Intention: On the pitch, teams can *make their intentions known* or *signal their intent* from the *outset*, often an attacking version of *setting their* **stall** *out*. Off the pitch, the word is often negated to *rebuff* transfer *speculation*: 'We have no *intention* of selling Emile'.

Interfering: When a player is not ***adjudged*** to be in an offside position, the debate is often whether he was or was not *interfering with play* (*with play* is often left understood): 'How could Sammy Lee not be *interfering* when he was lying face down in the eyeline of Phil Parkes?' Chairmen are also capable of *interfering* (*with **team affairs*** is often left understood too).

Inter-passing: 'Mark Hughes was delighted with Blackburn's *inter-passing* in the first half'. A term which sounds sophisticated even if it is gratuitous at first sight – between whom would you want passing to take place except team-mates? In effect, then, it is used to commend *retention* of the ball, especially if there is an interchange of passes among several players. Probably the usage reflects an appreciation of the *continental* style of play, but we have come across John Arlott employing it in the 1950s of English *legends*: 'The *inter-passing* of Haynes and Matthews laid the foundation of victory against Brazil'. In operatic Italy, the word *dialogo* can be brought into play, while a *duetto* constitutes a ***one-two***.

Intervention: Can serve as an alternative to goal, typically one that breaks the deadlock: 'But then came Channon's *intervention*'. At the other end, *interventions*, especially when *timely*, are made by defenders or, more rarely, goalkeepers. The corresponding verb is chiefly used of those who *intervene* to stop ***handbags*** from becoming a ***brawl***, be they referees or *peacemakers* (which is what such praiseworthy players are called in these circumstances).

In the hole: 'King opted for the 4-5-1 formation once again with Sammy Igoe *in the hole* just behind *lone* *striker Parkin'.* Parkin may well have been *ploughing a lone furrow* in this game given the way his side had been *set up*, but the *hole* in question has not been hollowed out by his *tireless running.* An elusive tactical term, the phrase is ubiquitous now, whether the player in the ***withdrawn*** *role* is operating behind two strikers or one. It may also be applied retrospectively. For example, although he will have found some other way of describing the *hole* at the time, Bobby Robson reminisces on his UEFA Cup tactics in the modern idiom: 'We played with two strikers at Ipswich, and with little Eric Gates *in the hole* just behind them'.

In their faces: 'We need to *get in their faces* and play at a fast ***tempo***, just as we did against Leeds'. An expression which may have come from the drill-yard when a sergeant-major is barking at his subordinates. When transferred to sport it is the subordinates who need to *get in the faces* of their superiors in order to have any chance of winning. Although more natural in rugby, the phrase has become a rallying cry for underdogs in football, thanks to the increasing ***gulf*** in ***class*** between the Premiership and the lower leagues (not to mention the increasing *gulf* within the Premiership itself).

In there: Common shorthand in radio commentary to indicate who has come up for a set piece: 'Ferdinand's *in there*, Neville's *in there*, Silvestre's *in there*'. But sometimes the *there* can denote an area more painful than the penalty box: 'Fabregas left his foot *in there* and the linesman did not see it'.

Introduction: Whether for a team or a player, usually a chastening experience. The favourite accompanying adjective is *harsh*, as witnessed by: 'It was a *harsh introduction* to the Premiership'. Can be used more neutrally of a substitution: 'After the *introduction* of Wilcox, Leeds had a bit more ***width***'.

Invitation: A usage which chides a defence for being so *schoolboy* as to have *gift-wrapped* a chance for a *natural goalscorer*, and simultaneously compliments the striker for his *poacher's instincts*: 'Godden could only parry the shot and Greenhoff needed no *second invitation*'.

Ironically: Study the following three examples:

'*Ironically*, after beating Preston in the previous round, Mick Harford's men now face another round trip to Lancashire';

'Ref Kim Milton Nielsen is handing Beckham the *matchball*. *Ironically*, Becks was sent off by him last time they met';

'Dickov, released by Man City last year, *ironically grabbed* the first goal for Leicester against them'.

In none of these instances is *irony*, invoked in football at the hint of the slightest coincidence or the smallest twist of fate, really present. Let's examine these situations again and imagine circumstances in which they could be called *ironic*. Maybe they could conceivably be thus counted if:

Harford had, as a psychological ploy, said to his men before playing Preston: 'I'm telling you, if you dare lose this game, I'm going to discipline you by putting you back on the coach next week to make the long trip to Lancashire all over again';

Kim Milton Nielsen had on the previous occasion sent Beckham off for picking the ball up and holding it in his hands during the match;

The manager who released Dickov had explained in so doing that he didn't score enough goals. A player-manager, he himself was the beaten goalkeeper. And his wife was born in Leicester. And she was going out with Dickov.

See also *literally*.

-ite: The suffix *-ite*, in common with usage in political language, indicates allegiance rather than resemblance (see *-esque*). For some reason it seems to be more common in the north: *Koppite, Spireite, Wednesdayite.*

J

Jack Walker: 'Dave Whelan is Wigan's *very own Jack Walker*'. Since the 1990s, whenever a wealthy British businessman begins to *bankroll* a football club, he may be compared to the Lancashire steelman who bought his team the ***Premiership***. In this millennium, a Siberian oilman has provided journalists with a new paradigm, although things do not always go to plan in the Nationwide South: 'Karl Williams played the *Abramovich role* at AFC Hornchurch until his double-glazing company went bust'.

Jet-heeled: Seen occasionally in programme notes as a synonym for *quick*. Perhaps only in our imagination, but used particularly of players called Jermaine.

Jigsaw: Once a manager has ***assembled*** his squad, he is often left searching for the *final* or *missing piece in the jigsaw*. You might think that the final piece of a jigsaw would be the easiest to place since there is only one space left for it. But not in football.

Job: There are a number of situations in which a *job* gets done in football. For example, when a player is asked to play out of position and is concerned not to let the team down: 'Keane prefers to play in midfield but can *do a job* for United in defence'. Or again, when a player succeeds in *marking* a key opponent *out of the game*: 'Horne *did a job on* Molby today and that was a contributing factor in our win'. We have also heard Andy Townsend say 'did a *job of work*' in this context. Third, whenever a shot *cannons off* it, a wall is said to have *done its job*. But the wall is *not* acknowledged to have 'done its job' when it induces the player taking the free kick to strike the ball wide or over. From which we deduce that the basic job description for a wall is to be hit by the ball. Meanwhile, *job done* is a phrase which greets any required achievement efficiently achieved, like a penalty *despatched* or a **professional** second leg performance to *seal* an aggregate victory.

Journey home: This is always lengthened disproportionately if the result has gone against you: 'It will be a *long journey home* to Bristol tonight for Gary Johnson *and his* **men**'. Whereas, if Gary's *men* had pulled off a spectacular victory *on the road*, the following, highly unlikely, scenario might be envisaged: 'The *red half* of Bristol will be *dancing in the streets* tonight'.

Journeyman: Although great players will make more and longer journeys than run-of-the-mill *pros*, the *journeyman* is one of the latter, moving forlornly between clubs in the lower divisions. The term denotes a player who has had *more clubs than Jack Nicklaus*, an old quip which (like *more bookings than Frank Sinatra*) is yet to be updated with reference to more contemporary figures. Those who think all this too pejorative may talk instead of, for example, '*well-travelled Imre Varadi*'. For a football club forced to **groundshare** while its stadium is renovated, use *nomadic*.

Just another player: When a team includes the son of a manager, both men will insist that he is *just another player*: 'Nigel is *just like any other player*: he

happens to have the number nine shirt on his back
because he is better than the number nine in the
reserves'. Should relatives be on opposing sides,
journalists will be unable to resist a reference to the
household, even if it is exceptional for adult men in
the same family to live under the same roof: 'Rio will
have **bragging rights** in the Ferdinand *household*';
'Harmony was preserved in the Little *household*'.

K

Kamikaze: Not many *kamikaze* pilots survived their
first mission, but the metaphor is still on active
service for a strategy of suicidal attack: 'While we
need three goals to win the tie, we mustn't go all
kamikaze early on and let in the *away goal*'. Managers
can also rewrite history when their team's defending
is too dreadful to be laughed off as *Keystone Cops*
stuff: 'Brian Laws lamented some *kamikaze* defending'. A self-inflicted goal caused by giving away possession needlessly can be described as an *act of
hara-kiri*.

Keep goal: The verb has a rather archaic flavour
these days, but may still be used without self-consciousness when you are talking about a goalkeeper
of a bygone era: 'Frank Swift *kept goal* for Man City
in those heady days'. Modern goalkeepers can however *keep* their team *in it* (a usage prompted also by
late goals in the cup). Some fans will prefer to use an
inexplicable plural: 'Arphexad's *in nets*'; 'Van
Breukelen's *in goals*'.

Keepy-uppy: The professional footballer has some
suspicion of this *piece of business*, even if he spends

a lot of the warm-up indulging in it, because the pace and urgency of a real game will not normally allow for such tricks, which are better reserved for an exhibition at half-time by Brazilian schoolgirls. Perhaps the other reason for the trade referring somewhat disparagingly to public displays of *ball-juggling* is that the usual volunteers for *keepy-uppy* are such custodians of the national game as Tony Blair, Michael Knighton, David Mellor and Mr Woo.

Keystone Cops: A ready allusion when a defence is *at **sixes** and **sevens***: 'That was *Keystone Cops stuff* from Vale there'. *Comedy* can also be used adjectivally in this way: '*Comedy* defending from Craddock and Thorne'. But note that when the blame lies squarely and obviously with one player, above all if a goal-keeping *clanger* should occur, and it seems cruel to laugh, comedy tends to give way in conventional commentaries to embarrassment or even sympathy: 'You have to *feel for* the **lad** there, Des'.

Kick: The basic action in the game, but too basic to be a significant word in reporting on it. Passing, crossing and shooting are simply more purposeful, so that the word *kick* is required only in compounds like *over-head kick* and *bicycle kick*, having become virtually redundant with *penalty* and *corner*. Only the goal-keeper's use of his feet can systematically be referred to as *kicking*, while attempts to *kick* your opponents *off the **park*** have nothing to do with the ball. Meanwhile *Kicker* might appear to be a good English word, except that it provides the title of the main German paper devoted to football, as well as featuring in some of that nation's clubnames (*Kickers Offenbach* is the sprightliest example). There is nothing comparable in English, unless you count Mark Smith's polemic against the football authorities trampling on flair in

his *Kicker Conspiracy* – but then Mark Smith is used
to playing in Germany.

Kick-off: Tends to be used more as the time approaches
than during or after a game. You would always say:
'Just ten minutes to *kick-off…*', but ten minutes *into the
game* it would be unusual to say 'Ten minutes after
kick-off…'. *Kick off* as a verb is also appropriated to
describe the outbreak of football-related violence, often
with a similar sense of anticipation: 'It looks like it
could *kick off* over there any minute'.

Kick-start: A phrase used by managers when they
hope a good performance will **turn round** *their
fortunes:* 'I really hope this win will *kick-start* our
season'. More applicable than **restart**, which serves
instead to indicate the resumption after half-time,
and more probable than *jump-start*, although this is
potentially the more appropriate image for teams
whose form is *spluttering*.

Kill off: What goalscorers do to cup-ties: 'It was
left to McFadden to *kill off* the tie with his second of
the afternoon'. It is rarer, at least in reportage, to see
such an unsentimental phrase applied directly to the
losing team: 'The third goal has finally *killed*
Scunthorpe *off*'.

Killer ball: Tends to be employed in a critical way to
highlight what a team lacks: 'They've played **pretty**
enough stuff *in front of them* but there's no *killer ball*'.
For concerns of the same order, you can refer to **final
ball** and **end product**.

Knock the ball about: A phrase with connotations
of knockabout for teams happy to *knock the ball about*,
or simply *knock it about*, if they are winning easily
and able to indulge in **exhibition stuff**.

L

Lackadaisical: An emphatic euphemism for 'lazy' or 'lacking concentration'. Reserved for individual defenders or the **back four** as a unit. In football, the variant form *lacksadaisical* also seems to be allowed, perhaps by contamination with *lax*.

Lacklustre: Can be said of any individual or team *display*, but particularly of flat, lifeless home performances. Nicely weighted in this summing-up by Barry Fry: 'We were toothless, *lacklustre* and complacent'.

Lads: 'We've got a *great set of lads* here at Millmoor and you can begin to see that in our play'. Not quite such a common term as in the 1980s (it is hard to think of Arsène Wenger referring to *the lads* rather than *my players*). In the singular, *lad* tends to be used for somebody who has been unfortunate or who has shown his fighting spirit: 'You have to feel sorry for the *lad*'; '*All **credit*** to the *lad* for coming back from that injury'.

Land: 'We've *landed* Lazio'. What star-struck smaller teams say when they are *paired* with one of the **big boys** in a tournament.

Last man: Since the change in the laws, the shorthand for a defender who is the last line of defence and could therefore risk dismissal if he illegally *denies* the opposition a *clear **goalscoring opportunity***. Used less insistently of the final defender when marginal offside decisions are being analysed.

Last-gasp: Often said of goals (equalisers or winners rather than **consolations**): 'Having led for much of the game, England were *stunned* by Zinedine Zidane's *last-gasp* free kick'. In this particular match there was one more *gasp* to come. For desperate clearances, the more likely expression is *last-ditch*.

Latch onto: A classic expression for a forward either making a good connection or running on to a pass. When they *meet* crosses they tend to do so with their heads.

Late run: The adjective *late* here designates a *well-timed run* (often those of attacking midfielders) spotted too *late* by defenders, so that it works almost like a transferred epithet: 'Scholes's *late run* and *emphatic finish* wrapped up the points for *United*'.

League: Ten years ago when Juventus, Real Madrid or Ajax won the *league* they won the *league*. Now, thanks to Channels 4 and 5 (and Ryanair), people talk only of *Serie A*, *La Liga*, *Eredivisie* and so on. Similarly, Francis and Souness may reminisce about missing out on winning the title with Sampdoria and dream of managing them to another *scudetto*. Only Alex Ferguson seems to stick to the old style, although he pronounces the word 'weague'.

Left to right: It is a topos of radio commentary that you will start a half by saying that 'Oldham Athletic are playing from *left to right* as we look'. Yet, unless you give the location of the commentary box, the information is not necessarily useful. For some reason, when referring to the visiting fans or a landmark near the ground, radio commentators always seem to say '*away* to our left' rather than just 'to our left'.

Left-sided: A phrase used much more commonly than *right-sided*, because of the premium on *left-sided* players (and in recent years because of a perceived deficiency on England's *left side*). Perhaps because of political correctness, there seem to be fewer references to *left-footers* than *left-sided players* nowadays. But, for *left feet*, see **educated** and **trusty**.

Legislate: 'You just can't *legislate* for a ricochet like that'; 'There's no *legislating* against such an **outrageous** piece of skill'. But you can, it seems, *legislate* for how managers console themselves publicly in such circumstances.

Legs: There are 46 of them on the pitch when the game gets under way, but the occasions are comparatively few for reporting on their activity. When a defender tackles an opponent unfairly from behind, he *takes his legs away*. Or if a winger *has the legs* on his full back, he is just plain quicker. But while footballers can be routinely described as having *good feet*, we have not come across a reference to 'fast legs'. Instead, the most predictable context in which *legs* are likely to appear is when there is a late substitution: 'It may be time for Graham to think about *fresh legs* at this stage in the game'.

Lesser nations: The **minnows** among international teams, once a constituency as recognisable and as pitiable as the minor counties in cricket. Games against them in a qualifying group provided an opportunity to *improve* your *goal difference*. But now managers or pundits wary of an upset often use the less condescending *so-called lesser nations*. It has also become conventional for such managers to observe, with some nostalgia, that there are *no easy games now*.

Lesson: Always a **football** or *footballing lesson, handed out* by the opposition. See also **examination**.

Level: Especially in the phrase *at this level* and typically for admonitory effect: '*At this level* you'd expect to hit the target every time from that distance'. *Leveller*, meanwhile, can be found as a synonym for *equaliser*, as well as describing what the **playing surface** is likely to become on a **Wednesday night in Rochdale**.

Lifeline: As opposed to a **consolation**, which as a general rule can arrive only when you are three goals adrift, teams are thrown a *lifeline* at two-down when they score with a few minutes left. This invariably *makes things interesting*: 'Kevin Horlock made it 2-1 to throw City a *lifeline*'.

Likes of: Like **your**, used to connect rarefied lists of star players or teams: 'Of course we want to be playing in the Premiership against *the likes of* Chelsea, Arsenal and United'.

Limp off: Shorthand for a player withdrawing through **injury**, even if the *knock* is not actually causing him to limp. Players still actually on the pitch are very rarely described as *limping*. Rather, they are said to be *not moving freely*, having a **problem** or *carrying a knock*. They only start *limping* as they actually *come off* the field of play.

Line-up: Useful alternative to *team*, particularly in pre-match discussion, when you want to pay more than usual attention to its component parts or to the formation its members might take up. Then, as the live commentary begins, you can switch over to the verb: 'Ipswich *line up* then with Sivell in goal…'.

Link: In the summer months of years ending in odd numbers (no World Cups or European Championships, in other words) transfer *speculation* is all the

more rife. 'Rivaldo has been *linked* with Tottenham' is
the standard formulation. Usually this means there is
no *link* other than that rumoured by the paper where
you see this written. Easier to corroborate is *link play*,
often *good **old-fashioned** link play*, responsible for
connecting defence with attack.

Literally: Like ***ironically*** and *massively*, massively
overused in football. Whether they say '*literally* the
last kick of the game' or 'he *literally* cut him in half',
there is no guarantee that they mean it, although the
first of these examples has to be truer than the second.

Loan: A few rules apply here: players are not described
as *loaned* to another team but are *sent* or *farmed* out *on
loan* (the latter phrase is probably better suited to cases
involving players *out of **favour***). Indeed, the term *loan
out* is likely to be used less of a manager sub-leasing a
player than of a ***busy*** midfielder as keen to get the ball
back as he is to move it on: 'Teams need players like
Prutton who are good at *loaning* the ball *out*'.

Local hero: Commentators too need to prove themselves *at international **level*** these days and there are
formulae which attest to their serious homework or
proper acclimatisation: 'Some of the home fans I
talked to in the restaurant last night rate their strik-
ing pair highly'. While commentating on a match
abroad, you do not want to be caught out if the local
cameraman dwells for an eternity on some venerable
figure in an overcoat who looks like he could never
have been a footballer. This personage could turn out
to be a *legend*, if not quite an ***ambassador***. He can be
called a *local hero*, but usually in a qualified way:
'Krankl's still something of a *local hero by all
accounts*'. Then you may add a statement like: 'They
still talk about that winning strike of his against
Luxembourg *in these parts*'.

Locker: 'Junichi just has so many tricks in his *locker*'. American sports have not infiltrated football to the degree that *dressing rooms* can ever become 'locker rooms', but the lexicon does admit a figurative *locker*, where special accomplishments always seem to be stowed. The *silkier skills* can also come out from very traditional storage space: 'Henry's ***effort*** was another from his personal *top-drawer*, a lazy drag back past Pearce and *cosy* finish past Van der Sar'.

Long ball: *Long-ball game* is canonical, so much so that phrases like ***Route One*** now seem to be preferred. *Long balls* themselves can be *pumped* or *rained into* opposition *boxes* when they threaten to be effective, whereas ineffectual teams *resort to* or *fall back on* them.

Long time: 'The first goal was a *long time* coming'. While this possibly doesn't say much for what has gone before, the formula is used by commentators when a team scores after being on top. *A long time* is also the unit of measure for a football player's retirement: 'I try to savour every single moment because you are a *long time* retired in this game'.

Look for it: Typically in the imperfect tense: 'Owen *was looking for it*' – *it* being the foul that would earn a penalty or a free kick. This verb covers the contentious, ambiguous moment when a player who has *gone to ground* has neither obviously taken a ***dive*** nor unequivocally been fouled. It suggests, if this were possible, cheating within the rules of the game. When a player is said to *win a penalty*, similar suspicions are allowed to flicker.

Looking over their shoulders: This is done in anticipation, not of being tackled from behind, but of being *leapfrogged* in the table: 'Leicester City will still be *looking* nervously *over their shoulders* after a goalless draw away to Burnley'. Strangely, when **sucked** into the *relegation mire*, it always seems to be the whole team *looking over* their collective *shoulders*, unless a manager has a particularly devious chairman.

Look in the mirror: If defenders have been doing a lot of looking at one another of an evening, their angry managers generally exhort them to *look in the mirror*, or to *have a good look at themselves*.

Look out of place: Almost always negated to pay a compliment: 'Gabbidon has really *not looked out of place* at all in this *exalted company* in the first half'. If you want to extend this to praising a whole team which is *punching above its weight* against **quality** opposition, then it is common to hypothesise: 'You wouldn't know which was the lower-division team in this match if you had just turned up from *outer space*'. It is of course common knowledge in outer space that lower divisions exist.

Lost causes: 'We were **breaking** with purpose and *chasing lost causes*'. Some players have been praised for their enthusiasm in *chasing paper bags*, which are more material than *shadows*, but that's a futile pursuit too. You would think *chasing lost causes* would be plain daft but in football the inference is that persistence is always worthwhile. Compare **work-rate**.

Lottery of penalties: Commentators favour this combination of nouns particularly as extra time advances. However keenly anticipated, the *penalty shootout* tends to be preceded by the epithet *dreaded*. The same commentators who call penalties a *lottery* (one way of excusing England's successive failures from the spot) nevertheless invariably designate as the *hero* either the goalkeeper who makes the decisive save or the player who happens to be the one who takes the final winning penalty.

Lowly: 'Just 72 hours earlier we were congratulating the same players on their magnificent performance against Bognor. How then could they hit such a low against *lowly* Billericay?' This adjective seems to appear only in Christmas carols and football reports. When you wish to commend non-league or struggling teams for a *plucky* performance against stronger opponents, include the verb *belie* somewhere in the sentence: 'Wisbech Town belied their *lowly status* with a *battling* draw at Conference *giants* Telford'.

Lurk: Strikers often *lurk* by the far post or *loiter with intent* in the box, in keeping with their reputation for *nicking* goals, and sometimes also suggesting that they are in an offside position: 'Another *mix-up* in the Livi penalty area allowed the *lurking* Craig Dargo a shot on goal from 12 yards out'. The near post is considered far too conspicuous a place to *lurk*, even if you are amidst a *crowd* of players.

Luxury: 'Shinji Ono, who carried a *"luxury player" tag* at J-League club Urawa Reds, has become a *permanent fixture* in the Feyenoord side.' This is exemplary career progression, as long as Ono's wages have remained *lavish*. Other *luxuries* in football include missed penalties and star-studded benches.

M

Made himself big: The most common phrase to describe a goalkeeper's actions when he confronts an

opposing player bearing down on him in a ***one-on-
one***. Only used in the past tense after a save.

Magic: A word that has lately lost some of its *magic*,
but even the most seasoned commentator can still
anticipate *a moment of magic* which will *break the
deadlock*. At one time schoolyard graffiti might announce that 'West Ham are *magic*' – and perhaps
there was even a time when it was true. Now used
more of players than of teams to describe feats that
would be ***outrageous*** if performed by lesser mortals:
'Zola, the little *magician*, turned the game with a
moment of ***sublime*** skill'. *Sorcerer* can get an outing
in these circumstances ('that Zola was a Sardinian
sorcerer') but *wizard*, now anachronistic anyway (as
in '*wizard* of the *dribble*'), has been commandeered
for the foreseeable future by quidditch commentators.

Make no mistake: Synonymous with scoring, when
a routine chance presents itself to a *proven* striker:
'Shearer *made no mistake* from there'. Otherwise used
by managers and pundits to buy themselves time to
think of something to say: '*Make no mistake*, we'll be
absolutely focussed for Saturday'.

Make the most of it: Reserved for players, often
continentals, who ***go down*** as if they have been *shot*
or even *poleaxed*. Interchangeable with *make a meal
of it*. Such exponents particularly *deserve an Oscar*
or marks for *artistic impression* if they make a *remarkable recovery* as soon as the stretcher appears. See
also, for less ***blatant*** conduct of this sort, ***look for it***.

Make the shirt your own: To become an ***automatic*** selection in a particular position: 'Sansom
has *made* the number three shirt *his own*'. Now
that players can afford their own shirts which bear
names as well as numbers, this expression is less

common in club football, but it is still available for *international **duty***.

Makeshift: The standard adjective for a player deployed in an unfamiliar position: 'Dublin, the *makeshift* centreback'. Preferred to the adjective *acting*, although you can be an *acting manager* if you have not yet been appointed ***caretaker***. Also used of strike-forces or defensive units when a manager's resources are stretched. Compare ***recognised***.

Man: Always used in preference to other available nouns (like 'player' or 'footballer') after a sending-off which changes the *whole **complexion*** of a game: '*Down* to ten *men*, United quickly lost a second goal'; 'Nine-*man* Kidderminster held on for the remaining minutes'; 'With Trinidad and Tobago *reduced* to eight *men*, the game descended into farce'; '*Seven-man* Blades were clearly ***looking for*** an abandonment'.

Manager: Takes a variety of adjectives: ***wily***, *volatile*, *shrewd, canny, Scottish*. Further specification can be given in compound nouns which bring in the ***cheque-book***, the ***tracksuit*** and the ***caretaker***. Vernacular synonyms are *the gaffer, the guvnor, the boss*. *Management* tends not to be used unless it is qualified by an adjective, as in *man management*, or *top-**level** management*. Some players are *every manager's dream*, while *all managers will tell you* certain truisms about the game, including the fact that any *vote of confidence* in them from the chairman is *dreaded*.

Man-to-man: In modern parlance the locution is regarded as complete without the addition of *marking*: 'Koeman's now switched to *man-to-man* on Völler'; 'After the substitution Tottenham have reverted to *man-to-man* at the back'.

Many people's idea: How *pundits* present their own opinion as though it were the majority view: 'Sunderland struggled against a Forest side who are *many people's idea* of favourites for promotion'.

Mar: The verb favoured by commentators when embarrassed by the need to add to the business of reporting a match the account of a tragedy or serious misfortune – perhaps an earthquake has destroyed the South Stand or a star player has pulled a hamstring or crowd trouble has broken out (or all of the above have somehow caused one another). This verb *puts things into perspective*: 'United's win was *marred* by Pingel's broken leg'. A victory or match may likewise be *soured* in such cases. See also *gloss.*

Marching orders: *Given* to players who get a red card. A somewhat circumlocutory way of reporting a sending-off, though not as sublimely euphemistic as the *early bath*. *Expulsion* is a term used by reporters who have had a difficult childhood or a sabbatical reporting on Italian football.

Mark: Used narratively for timings in a game, with a margin of choice as to the preposition: '*On* the half-hour *mark*'; '*Around* the 70-minute *mark*'.

Marksman: Alternative, perhaps not as popular as it used to be, for *striker*. Goalscorers, particularly if they are in a *rich vein of form* or *among the goals* (a little phrase which neatly suggests the prowess of a striker accustomed to *finding the net*) can be said to be *on the mark again,* in an expression which combines the idea of a sharpshooter with being up to the mark.

Masterclass: *Maestro* used to be the prevailing term for a supreme player who could *orchestrate* the play in midfield. Perhaps the launch of the Austin car made *maestros* less of a *class* act. Now the *masterclass* is the prevalent metaphor, and the lessons of the great football virtuosi are given in real games rather than public training sessions: 'Zidane's *masterclass* in control, technique, application and skill was the dictionary definition of *sublime*'; 'Sacchi's Milan *turned on* a *masterclass* that night which will never be forgotten by those who witnessed it'.

Matchball: What a ball becomes when it is sponsored, taken home by a *hat-trick hero*, or offered at auction.

Mathematically: An adverbial favourite which recurs towards the end of every season. Popular in *situations* (which generally do not involve much mathematics) to denote a remote theoretical possibility: 'This is a giant step for Vale, Gary, but they're not *mathematically* safe yet'; 'After their defeat at the Reebok, Leeds are down, barring the *mother of mathematical miracles*'.

Maximum points: Three points or, more deliberately, *all three points*. 'Slaven's strike gave Boro *maximum points*'. The usage seems more justifiable when reporting pursuits like county cricket or ice-dancing, but is known to occur in football.

Mazy: Reserved exclusively for *runs* or *dribbles* by *tricky customers*: 'After a *mazy* run Huckerby *blasted* over the bar'.

Measured: Adjective applied especially to passes. Sometimes the tape measure, or *slide rule*, comes out and the pass is described as *inch-perfect*. Whereas crosses tend to be *pinpoint*. Shots from *point-blank* range are normally remarked upon when the goalkeeper makes a *reflex save*.

Meat and drink: In football circles this everyday cliché tends to be reserved for situations where attacking teams *play to the strengths* of the defenders: 'These *long balls* they keep *pumping in* are just *meat and drink* to Adams and Bould'. See also *bread and butter*.

Medical: Transfers always seem to be announced *subject to a medical*, a useful get-out clause for the acquiring team, and indeed for journalists who launch speculative exclusives. The other tabloid tactic consists of using the infinitive when announcing 'Zidane *to* sign for Spurs'. An indefinite future is masked by that useful little word.

Men: Note the journalistic fondness for saying 'Gary Johnson *and his men*' rather than Bristol City, more to vary the discourse than to evoke team spirit. There is a trend during cup draws for certain teams to be considered less prominent than their managers, no matter how old or dignified the club or how soon the current man in the *hot seat* might move on: '*Glenn Hoddle's* Wolves will play Arsenal'; '*Steve Cotterill's* Burnley have earned themselves a *plum tie* at Villa Park'. But never: 'Ernie Howe's Basingstoke'. Instead, non-league sides are patronised in a different way, being made *representatives* of their division: 'Emley, from the Rymans, will meet Chesterfield in the first round proper'.

Mentally: Adverb used with *prepared*, *ready* or *up for it*, sometimes *right* or *strong*, and even *gone* or *lost it*.

Merchant: A journalistic standby, as in these two phrases noted in the same edition of one paper: 'Owen is no longer simply a *head-down merchant*'; 'Arsenal have got to steel themselves against *the wind-up merchants*'.

Metatarsal: Before Beckham broke one of his *metatarsals*, most of us did not know we even had them. But he set a fashion followed more assiduously than some of his haircuts and tattoos. The *curse of the metatarsal* duly afflicted Rooney, Neville and Owen. In the past these players would simply have 'broken a bone' in their foot. But, now that it has become possible to watch operations on footballers in live web broadcasts, we are expected to have boned up a bit. Similarly, whereas a player would once routinely be described as going in for surgery on *gammy* or *dodgy* knees, the more informed jargon now includes *cruciate reconstruction* and *arthroscopic cartilage washing*.

Midfield: Historically there was no such thing as a *midfield* as long as a team possessed a self-respecting half-back line. Nowadays the *midfield* area is *packed* with its own *ever-willing* terminology. Individual *midfielders* can be variously described as *dervishes* or **dynamos**; they tend to be **busy**, honest, tenacious, versatile, workmanlike. They **prompt**, hustle, beaver away and work themselves into the ground. The *midfield* can be *flooded* or *swamped* by one team (or *congested* by both teams), so that there is *precious little space* there.

Midfield general: The player who *pulls the strings*, the man *at the heart of the action* or *of everything good* the team does. *Midfield generals* are supposed to be admired, but the term may hint at an ego or suggest some imperiousness, so a *midfield general* may be described less equivocally as *the playmaker*. A **pint-sized** and foreign *midfield general* may invite the designation *little Napoleon*. See also **instrumental**.

Minnow: Stocks of *minnow* in the FA Cup, its traditional spawning ground, seem to be dwindling and under threat. *Minnows* are barely sustainable in other

competitions and they rarely make their way into
international waters: 'Alongside the *usual suspects* in
the Champions League draw will be a *sprinkling* of
less *stellar dark horses*'.

Miskicks: There seem to be no gradations of *miskick*:
they are invariably *complete miskicks*. *Airshot* is occasionally imported from golf for the instances which
really are *complete miskicks*, and *miscue* from snooker
when players mishit a *potshot* on goal or **scuff** a clearance. More skilled footballers never 'cue' though.

Missile: Can be anything from a coin to a football
programme, from a bottle to a pig's head, provided
they are thrown by **so-called fans** onto the pitch.
Projectile is a more pompous alternative but somehow
less likely to convey a sense of moral indignation in
the commentator.

Mistimed: When managers defend a **tackle** by saying
it was *mistimed* and their player is *not that sort of **lad***,
you can be pretty sure it was *shocking*.

Mix: Towards the end of games where a side is *striv-
ing for the equaliser*, they are sometimes exhorted to
get it *into the mix* (or *mixer*), which is a synonym for
penalty box: 'Really Sunderland have to get the ball
back *into the mixer* if they want to get **something** out
of this game'.

Mortgage: Used almost invariably with the past conditional, thankfully for the speaker's financial well-
being: 'I would have *put my mortgage* on Shearer
scoring from the spot there, Clive'. The alternative
is *house*, but in modern Britain this amounts to the
same thing for most of us.

Mould: There are probably more managers than ever

who were once players, so it is now common to hear among older observers and commentators that, for instance, 'Wycombe are a team very much *in their manager's mould*'. A footballer who reminds you of a previous player may be described in such terms too: 'He's in the Ron Yeats *mould*'.

Mountain to climb: Manager-speak for a situation which has become even more grim than a *test of character*, when the side finds itself too many goals or points adrift for even an *unlikely comeback* to be possible: 'The second goal was *abysmal* and going two down gave us a *mountain to climb*'. Some managers have so little faith in their strikeforce that they expect to be using crampons the moment they fall behind: 'We can't keep going 1–0 down and *climbing mountains*'.

Movement: Teams or players can be characterised by good *movement* (*movement* is rarely mentioned in negative statements – see instead *square*, *static*), that ability to make runs into *space* and *shake your marker*. It is reserved in general for the *movement* of players running off the ball. *Moves well* tends to be combined with *for a big man*, as athleticism goes without saying otherwise.

Murder: In football, *murder* is not quite as terminal as you might think: 'We *murdered* them today, but couldn't quite *kill* them *off*'. Most frequently to be seen in press conference post-mortems after the opposition's corpse has been miraculously revivified when it should have been *put away*: 'We *murdered* them in the second half so for them to go up the other end and score was a *heart-breaker*'. Football parlance, perhaps aware of the fatigue to which its metaphors are subject, often gives you an adverb for free, as in 'we *absolutely murdered* them' or 'he *completely disappeared*'.

N

Naive: 'We were a bit *naive* going for the second goal and that's something we'll have to learn *at this level*'. Teams who are *defensively* or *tactically naive* will undoubtedly have their limitations ruthlessly *exposed* (although if they happen to win, their brave and uncomplicated approach will be like a *breath of fresh air*). Despite the fact that there are *no easy games* in modern international football, it is still taken as read that the *so-called lesser nations* are *tactically naive*, especially African teams – unless they have a European manager.

Narrowest of angles: Footballing hyperbole inflates a *narrow* or *tight* angle into the superlative: 'Gudjohnsen and Duff combined to *release* Hasselbaink, who beat Oakes *from the narrowest of angles*'. But the *narrowest of angles* would presumably involve a shot from the goal-line, so the phrase is not to be taken too literally.

Need: Many a game is said to *need a goal* by commentators in need of excitement: 'You're right, Mark, what this game really *needs* is a goal'. Generally, games *need a goal* only as long as it's 0-0. They never need additional goals (nor indeed anything else) though some matches simply *cry out* for someone to *put their foot on the ball* or for a bit of *quality* in the *final third*.

Neon lights: This is what players envisage when they *go for glory* with a spectacular *effort* on goal, ignoring the likelier *options*: 'I think Eric Young must have seen his name up in *neon lights* for a second there. Goal kick'. *Neon* is not compulsory in this phrase – you can use *bright* or drop the adjective completely.

Nerve: When a penalty-taker is said to have *kept* or *held his nerve*, he is understood to have scored: 'After Pearson was hauled down, Stewart *kept his nerve* from the spot'.

Net rash: Not a recognised medical condition, but football's colourful way of indicating that a goal-keeper has been picking the ball out of the net too often: 'Ian Walker's in danger of getting *net rash* the way we are playing'.

Neutral: There is no reason why a *neutral* should not also be a **purist**, but *the neutral*, as a rule invoked in the generic singular (although there may actually be as few as one neutral at British matches), tends by contrast to love as many goals as possible. The *neutral* will savour the *comedy defending* that leads to them too: 'It's great fun for the *neutral*, but heart-stopping for both sets of fans'.

Never: When a striker scores with a *simple **tap-in***, commentators promise: 'He'll *never* score an easier goal than that'. Not only is the future tense more expansive, but 'he'll *never* score' is also more secure than 'he has *never* scored' from qualification by any *anoraks* in earshot. The past tense is definitive, on the other hand, in those phrases with which the local **faithful** nod sagely to each other: 'He was *never* the same player after that injury'; 'They were *never* the same team after they sold Phelan'.

New-look: For some reason, football people tend not to say simply 'new'. There is instead always talk of a *new-look **line-up***, a *new-look* backroom team, a *new-look* Ewood Park. In the modern **Premiership**, training facilities always seem to be *state-of-the-art*.

No man's land: Like wicket-keepers, who are exhorted by the MCC coaching manual to stand right back or right up, goalkeepers faced with a teasing cross or through ball should either come right out to *claim* or not move off their line at all. Otherwise they will be caught in *no man's land*, when they should have *stayed at home*.

No slouch: When a commentator picks out a defender as *no slouch*, he will in fact be comparing the player unfavourably to the even quicker forward who has just beaten him to the ball: 'Harewood gave Phil Babb a three-yard start there, and Babb's *no slouch*'.

Nonchalant: The Brazilians are adored for their *nonchalant flicks*, but if the Blackpool number five *dilly-dallies* at the back he is being 'a bit too *nonchalant* there'.

No-nonsense: A *no-nonsense* midfield is unlikely to **over-elaborate**; a *no-nonsense* referee is usually quick to *reach for his cards*; a *no-nonsense* defender will tend to put the ball in *Row* **Z**.

Nonsense: Mildly censorious way of talking about **handbags**. *Antics* is another alternative, although this can be used more positively of the practical jokes played by **characters** in the **dressing room**.

Not fit: To be distinguished from *unfit* or *struggling for fitness*, in that it refers to moral suitability rather than physical condition. For example, when player A is *not fit* to *lace the boots* of player B (or *lace the drinks* if player B likes a tipple) a contrast in attitudes and professionalism is made extravagantly obvious. Another instance is *not fit* to *wear the* **shirt**, employed when a player has let down his side with a poor **work-rate**, a fit

of petulance or, worst of all, a gesture of defiance to
his own fans. An expression that momentarily came
to life when an Everton fan ran on to the pitch to
offer *lackadaisical* Alex Nyarko his shirt in
exchange.

Not the best: Understatement for 'very bad', not
to say *diabolical*: 'I'm not saying he meant to hurt
anyone but it was *not the best of tackles* and he will
see that on the video'. Occasionally a striker's *effort*
on goal is described as *not one of his best* (compare
disappointed).

Nothing: Often preferred to *nil* north of the border,
just as *north of the border* is often preferred to *Scotland*
by commentators south of it. Hugh Johns also preferred 'one-*nothing*' during his ITV commentaries of
the 1970s, perhaps to avoid the 'one-*nil*' catchphrase
of his BBC rival David Coleman. Individual skill can
sometimes *conjure* a goal *out of nothing* (compare
nowhere). Whereas a *nothing ball*, the result of *hit
and hope*, is a disappointing end to the move.

Nothing with kids: 'And so Arsenal's youngsters
reached the last eight of the competition for the third
consecutive year. They have *won nothing with kids*
yet, but it is still an impressive feat'. The allusion here
is to Alan Hansen's celebrated remark on the opening
day of a season when *Fergie's Fledglings* went on to
win the league (after the *Busby Babes* any nickname
for a young team must be alliterative). A manager
actively favouring *youth* can always cover his position
by dropping out Hansen's adage.

Nouveau fan: Not really that common a label, the
term mimicking the sort of language such a fan would
himself use, while most supporters would come up
with blunter names for him. But its Frenchness is

apposite, partly because of the enviable success of the
French national side or, if you prefer, *les Bleus* (compare *League*) in recent years, and partly because the
French language corners the market when it comes to
bourgeois, *parvenus* and *arrivistes* of different sorts.
The middle classes have always gone to football in
Britain, and the term is levelled not at them, but at
people who, while professing an interest in football,
think *Tuscany* when they hear *Villa*, *Rugger* when
you say *Brian Moore*, *Good* when they see *Baddiel*.

Nowhere: Whence gifted players come up with
chances: 'Kanouté produced a goal from *nowhere* with
a stunning strike'. Where players are sometimes going
before they are fouled: 'You have to say Scholes was
going nowhere really until Taylor *needlessly* caught him'.

Nutmeg: A classic trade term whose derivation is
a matter of some debate. *Nutmegs* could either be
rhyming slang for 'legs' and the phrase for putting the
ball through them came into vogue by association, or
nutmegs is a slang term for 'testicles' which feel the
draught as the ball goes under them, or again *nutmegs*
is a contraction of 'not through my legs'. Alternatively,
to *nutmeg* in nineteenth century slang was 'to deceive'.
When abbreviating, use the second syllable – 'Yorke
megged the keeper' – unless you are describing a
bust-up, when *nutted the keeper* might be appropriate
after all.

O

Obscurity: Noun preceded by either *non-league* or
mid-table. A player *languishing* in this condition will
hope to be *plucked* from it.

Occasion: When a manager formulates a *game plan* against certain opposition or *keeps tabs* on a player, he will claim to have had them **watched** on a *number of occasions*, the phrase quietly suggesting that he presides over an outstanding *scouting network*. As an alternative to talking about the *big-match* **atmosphere**, commentators can remark on *a real sense of occasion*. Players do not suffer from stage fright but can let the *occasion get to them* in a dauntingly big match. And when Italian *imports* translate themselves in post-match interviews, *occasion* becomes a synonym for *chance*.

Odd goal: 'Thistle won by the *odd goal* in five'. Superfluous, circumlocutory way of saying 3-2, usually to add variety when **rounding up** a series of results. Rarely used for other **scorelines**.

Of age: A phrase emphasising a player's precocious talent. Note how prodigies such as Ian Snodin are invariably described as *only 18 years of age* rather than 'only 18 years old' or 'only 18'. In the same vein commentators can purr over the maturity that can be shown for *one so young*: 'The Doncaster **starlet** has *an old head on young shoulders*'.

Of all people: 'In the famously uncharitable Charity Shield of 1974, Bremner and Keegan were separated by Norman Hunter, *of all people*'. When *cloggers* turn peacemakers, forwards take to *defensive duties* or perhaps a defender finds himself **one-on-one** with the keeper in a moment of **total football**, this is the requisite phrase: 'That's Shearer *of all people* hacking it off the line'. The tone of astonishment is such as might be appropriate for a sudden appearance by Princess Michael of Kent in the penalty box. But when, *of all people*, a ballboy made a goal-line clearance during a Greek league match, the degree of incredulity was no doubt warranted.

Off the back: 'Marcus Bent is absolutely livid. He's made a tremendous run *off the back* of Pena'. The striker's art consists of staying *on the **shoulder*** of his marker, to avoid being caught offside, and to make his runs *off the back* of the defender when it is safe to expect a through ball.

Off the pitch: Can be a more telling dimension than *on the pitch*. Frequent in player profiles to warn you that the secrets of a private life are about to be revealed: '*Off the pitch*, Lee likes nothing better than to **relax** with steady girlfriend Alicia over a glass of wine' – it is reassuring to know that he does not do this on the pitch. Often also a convenient way of criticising a player's conduct by inference: 'He's such a polite, pleasant person *off the pitch*'. The two phrases can combine, particularly when there is talk of **well-documented** problems: 'It's been a difficult twelve months *on and off the pitch* but everyone at the **football club** has worked hard and stuck together'.

Office: In one of those phrases which suggest footballers are professionals, just doing a job like the rest of us, defeats are sometimes rationalised as *bad days at the office*. Perhaps more understandable when used of **officials**: 'Paul Jewell complained that nothing happened to referees if they have a string of *bad days at the office*'.

Officials: There are now four of these, known collectively as the *match officials* in club programmes, but it is only the *fourth official* who is habitually called an *official*. The referee presumably is the first *official*, his linesmen, sorry *assistant referees*, jointly second *officials*, but they are never described as such.

Offside: Always a *trap*, and if ineffective, usually *sprung* or, more plainly, *beaten*. See also **yard**. *Onside* (often abbreviated to *on*) is normally worth talking about only if there is a *suspicion* it was not: 'I think Venison was just *playing* Bright *on* there, Mike'.

Old boy: Although the days when Old Etonians won the FA Cup are behind us, the public-school phrase may still be used of players *renewing their acquaintance* with former clubs: 'Liverpool *old boy* Robbie Fowler goes back to his old *stamping ground* today'. The term does say something more than merely *former* or *ex*, insofar as it implies a youthful association and some lingering mutual affection. For these reasons, although Leeds was a subsequent former club of his, Fowler would not be described as a 'Leeds old boy'.

Old-fashioned: Sometimes preceded by *good*. Reserved as a rule for the description of *centre-forwards* who have teeth missing and can only head the ball (or goalkeeper). Used also with the nouns *shoulder-charge, mudbath, cup-tie* and *free-for-all*.

On fire: 'Yang Chen has been absolutely *on fire* for Shenzhen Jianlibao'. Only strikers seem to ignite in this way – however brilliant the performances of a defender, it would be irregular to say 'Michael Dawson has been on blazing form all season'. This is partly because the confidence a goal brings to a forward can seem to *spark off* a chain reaction, and partly because defenders are naturally thought of as fire-fighters. Managers can always be left *fuming* though.

On the ball: A defunct exhortation, commemorated in the title of some television programmes and in a timeless (and tuneless) anthem at Carrow Road, if City are playing well.

On the night: A phrase that distinguishes a result over one leg from the aggregate score, often in contrast to it: 'Although it only made it 2-1 *on the night*, Speedie *levelled the tie* with a firm right foot shot'; '1-0 to Rangers *on the night* then, but they go out *on aggregate*'. Preferred to 'on the day', even if it was an early kick-off in Vladikavkaz.

On the rebound: The orthodox phrase for a score following an initial save from a penalty but, perhaps surprisingly, seldom used in open play. Strikers are more likely to *follow* up or hit the net at the *second time of asking*.

On our travels: Perhaps the commonest way of saying *away from home*, particularly in the special pleading of managers' programme notes: 'After so many near misses *on our travels* this season, it was nice that everything came right for us at the Riverside'. *On the road* is a variant, even in these days of domestic air-flights: 'It was a battling performance and that was great to see, because we have been labelled softies *on the road*'.

One-on-one: A *situation* in which an opposing player bears down on the goalkeeper. The phrase is almost never used for *individual* **battles** elsewhere on the pitch. However, you might hear: 'It was *four-on-two* for a moment in that last Wolves break'.

One thing on his mind: A striker with *predatory instincts* should not be denounced as *selfish* once he has ignored all his available team-mates, as long as he ends up scoring. Indeed, if the *goal-hungry* individual is acknowledged to be a *natural-born striker*, commentators will remark, with more than a hint of admiration: 'Hasselbaink had only *one thing on his mind* there'. Whereas if Hasselbaink *blazes* over, he should, of course, have got his *head up*.

One-two: If successful almost always *neat* or *quick*; if unsuccessful described as *intended* or **ambitious**. The synonym *wall pass* is becoming obsolete.

One-way traffic: The opposite of **end-to-end stuff.** As so often in commentary you are made to notice it has been *one-way traffic* when something happens at the other end: 'It was all *one-way traffic* in this one until Shrewsbury sneaked away to *nick* a last-minute winner'. Even the proverbial **coach and horses** can sometimes be travelling in an unexpected direction.

Only as far as: 'Beasant *clears, only as far as* Bracewell'. In radio commentaries, where this phrase is especially common, the listener will have no idea how far this is. The distance is of no importance, the phrase serving only to indicate that possession has changed hands.

Operate: Generally applied to wide players who can **switch** flank, as in 'Giggs is now *operating* on the right'. But also common to describe the role of the 1s in a 4-1-2-1-2 – 'Batty is *operating* just in front of the **back four**'; 'Scholes is *operating* in a **withdrawn** *role* just behind the front two'.

Opportunism: Off the pitch you would not want to be known for *opportunism*, but strikers may be praised for it: 'The game was heading for a **stalemate** when a typical moment of *opportunism* from Garner gave Rovers the points'. An *opportunity* is a synonym for *chance* and may be *taken with both hands*, even by footballers.

Opposite number: Archaic reference, from the days before **squad numbers**, to an opponent in the corresponding position.

Options: Widely employed to indicate the choices available in open play – 'he had *options* ahead of him but chose to shoot' – and sometimes also at a free kick: 'Redknapp and Anderton are the *options* here'. Players are also excused a *wayward pass* if they had *no options* or *no out-ball*. Perhaps the most standard usage of all is to describe what a manager has available to him if he wants to *make a **change***: 'Asaba, Hartenberger and Bernal: they're the *options*, Alan'.

Organise: On construction sites *walls* simply get built, but on football pitches they have to be *organised* by keepers, which is why they are not always ready on time: 'With David Seaman still *organising his wall*, Harte *fired* in the free kick to *stun* the Highbury crowd into silence'.

Orthodox: While *recognised* is usually qualified by a negative in football parlance, as in 'not a *recognised* striker', *orthodox* is usually positive in effect. It seems to be employed primarily of defenders: 'They've brought on Barton, a more *orthodox* right-back'. *Unorthodox*, on the other hand, pertains to goalkeepers when they have ***improvised a clearance***.

Out-and-out: As a rule used adjectivally with the noun *striker* to designate a ***no-nonsense*** centre-forward: 'Ellington is being deployed as an *out-and-out striker* whereas he used to play in a more ***withdrawn*** role at Bristol Rovers'. More common in modern times with the frequent use of the *lone striker*, *out-and-out* is used to distinguish a player who would always take this role rather than *play **in the hole***.

Outfit: Nothing to do with *kits*, but a synonym for team or club, typically coupled with a handy geographical reference: 'It has been a bad week for the Cheshire *outfit*'.

Outlay: Generic term for a manager's expenditure, often with a censorious tone: 'Recent performances failed to justify Hoddle's summer *outlay*'.

Outmuscle: New-fashioned word for the **old-fashioned** forward who comes off best in a physical encounter: 'Lawrence thumped the ball narrowly over the bar after *outmuscling* Leighton Baines'; 'Hulse scored the winner and generally *outmuscled* the Norwich defence'. Perhaps centre-halves are less uncompromising than they used to be: 'In my day Micky Droy at Chelsea was another monster of a guy with *muscles in his spit*'.

Outnumbered: Not used so much when teams are *reduced* to ten men, but to indicate a tactical problem where a side is apparently being *outnumbered in midfield* or, say, a full back unlucky enough to be *playing behind* David Ginola keeps finding himself *outnumbered* on the left flank.

Outrageous: In Britain, it is quite possible to be outraged by skill. Skill is *outrageous* when unexpected or extravagant. Dummies in particular may be *outrageous*, whereas bad conduct is never so described but should instead be characterised as *disgraceful*.

Outstretched leg: When a defender pulls off a superb sliding tackle or clearance, the limb that effects it almost becomes amputated from the player in the commentator's eyes: 'Cambridge were saved only by the *outstretched leg* of O'Shea'. Note likewise that decapitation can seem to occur when, in a standard phrase, it is said 'the game was stopped for two minutes after a *clash of heads*'.

Over the top: Denotes a *shocking* tackle (*of the ball* is understood) where the player has deliberately *gone in* with **studs** *up* in an attempt to injure his opponent.

Over-elaborate: Adjective enlisted whenever a *pretty* passing move has failed or a team has missed an opportunity to *test* the keeper by taking one touch too many. One of those compounds (see also *sky-high*) favoured by football parlance, even when the adjective 'elaborate' would do. An elaborate or intricate move, when it succeeds, will tend to be described as *well-worked*.

Overnight: When teams have pressed the *self-destruct button* and suffered a heavy or unexpected defeat, managers are very quick to point out: 'We haven't suddenly become a bad team *overnight*'. Their *long-suffering* supporters may sometimes be forgiven for retorting that the team has indeed been useless for years. Furthermore, no manager or coach would ever admit to his side having suddenly become 'a good team overnight', unless he felt the need to comment on their behaviour in the team hotel.

Overplay: 'The aim of this Northamptonshire FA paper is about raising the awareness of coaches who have direct contact with our best young players to the risks of *overplay*'. Technical trade term for *burn-out*, a particular issue for *Academy prospects* still growing into their frames. At more senior levels, managers playing *mind games* can try not to *overplay* the importance of an **occasion**, at least until they have won. The word can also be used of teams who are not *direct* enough: 'More hard work must be done so that we take the right **options** in attack and not *overplay*'.

Overworked: Referring to keepers and defences under pressure. It is tempting to protest that goalkeepers and defenders are paid (some say overpaid)

to *do their jobs*, but the implication is that they are
not being properly *protected* by the rest of the side.

Own goal: *Own goals* tend, like deflections, to be
described with sympathy for those who fall victim to
them. Often therefore preceded by the adjectives *freak*
or *bizarre* even when 'incompetent' or 'stupid' might
come more readily to mind: 'Lee Martin's *bizarre own
goal* gifted Montpellier a first-half lead'.

P

Pace: An *asset* which is described by a variety of
adjectives: *blistering*, **electric**, *frightening*, *lethal*,
lightning, *scorching*, *searing*. When a player is very
quick, he has *pace to burn*; when he is only *quicker
than he looks*, he can show *deceptive pace*. When *pace*
means **tempo** it is more likely to be qualified as *fran-
tic* or *frenetic*. In this context, the *pace* of a game can
be *dictated* or *stepped up*, and an *injection* of *pace* can
be provided whether by a player himself or by a
manager putting him on. *Pacy* tends to appear more
in player profiles than live commentary, while we
found a reference in an old *Shoot* to '*quicksilver* Tony
Woodcock'.

Pacesetter: A discreet way of suggesting that the
leaders near the beginning of the season might
be provisional. Indeed, the word *early* often appears
as a qualifier: 'Barry Town, the division's *early pacesetters*, came a cropper at Afan Lido on Saturday'. On
the other hand, *pacesetters* will not necessarily always
give way to those who are thought to be able to stay
the course, as they do obligingly in athletics. Never
say 'pacemakers' in footballing contexts, unless

you are a manager joking about the *pressures* of the job or a journalist writing a feature on the *Kop Choir*.

Parity: A stylised way of describing an equaliser, almost invariably with the verb *restored* in the passive voice: '*Parity* was *restored* five minutes later when Cottee *sneaked in* at the far post to *convert* a cross from Devonshire'.

Park: Teams may be *played off* it or, conversely, they may enjoy a *stroll* in it, but applicable also as a synonym for *pitch*: 'McGrain's the most experienced player on the *park*'. Particularly common in Scottish parlance, perhaps because of the relative frequency of *Park* in Scottish stadium addresses.

Part: Vanquished teams often *play their part* in games admired by the **neutral**. Commentators indicate that an injury will result in a substitution by saying: 'It looks like Immel will *take no further part*'. Meanwhile, there are certain things that should have *no part* in *the game of football*: for example racist abuse, or spitting, or any other *disgraceful* **scenes**. Strangely, these are not counted among football's **cardinal sins**. Indeed, much unsavoury behaviour seems to be all *part and parcel* of the game, especially under the categories of the *bust-up* and the **tap up**.

Partners: An attacking duo, intent on *poaching* goals *for fun*, may be described as *partners in crime*. A pair of centre-backs will never develop the same frisson of notoriety, but when they develop a good *understanding* with one another they can be said to *strike up* a *great partnership* at the *heart* of the defence.

Part-timers: The fact that a team may be *semi-professional* is usually emphasised when they have

sprung or potentially can spring a shock: 'The *part-
timers* from the Faroe Islands are giving Austria a
real fright'. Often the professions of individual players are referred to, especially if it offers the chance for
alliteration: 'The plasterer from Plaistow pounced on
a poor clearance as the Daggers got off to a ***dream
start***'.

Passage: 'After a *thrilling passage of play*, the game
returned to tripe'. This example from Rick Broadbent
is tongue-in-cheek, but it is possible to talk about
passages of play in football, even if the phrase lends
itself more to rugby where there are clear phases of
possession. Teams successful in cup-ties formally
book their passage into the next round.

Pedigree: The FA Cup commands its own lexicon.
For example, those clubs or players who have been
lucky enough to taste *cup glory* build up a reputation
for their *cup pedigree*. Neither of these nouns sits as
happily with 'league'.

Peg: Synonym for *leg*, particularly in the Scottish
vernacular.

Penalty: If you are still in Scotland, you may want to
award the *penalty kick* its full title according to the
laws. *Penalties* tend to be *hotly **disputed***, even if the
referee has *no hesitation* in *pointing to the spot*. This
is a standard way of saying that a penalty has been
given, whereas the verb *penalise* is used only for
infractions outside the box: 'Merk's *penalised* the
Blues for ***dissent*** by moving the free kick forward'.

Per cent: The unit of measure for ***work-rate*** and
commitment. If managers want real ***industry*** they
ask for 110, 200 or even 1,000 *per cent effort*. ***Fifty-
fifties*** are tackles where both players will certainly be

expected to give at least 100 *per cent*. *Good percentage play* is an expression perhaps more appropriate in tennis or golf, but it can be used in football to describe a *safety-first option* by a defender or cautious tactics in general.

Per cent record: Once the season gets under way, as long as teams are winning all their matches, they enjoy a *100 per cent record* (110 per cent is unfortunately not available in this context). But those sides who lose all their matches are never correspondingly saddled with a '0 per cent record'. That would just be too unsparing. Nevertheless, other formulae can seem to suggest that it's hardly worth their getting out of bed: 'Clydebank, *pointless on their travels*, make the short trip to Boghead Park with no fresh injury worries'.

Perfectly good goal: Those who score a *perfectly good goal* do not score at all, for this is the formula when a team has a legitimate strike *ruled out*: 'Middlesbrough deserved the win – especially as they had a *perfectly good* Frank Queudrue *goal* chalked off in the first half'.

Perform: Often employed in the negative to indicate a poor team or individual effort: 'We just didn't *perform* at all on the day'. Conversely, players who *perform **week in week out*** are singled out for praise. An accompanying adverb never seems necessary.

Period: Although extra-time is structured as a match in miniature, it is traditional to refer to its halves as *periods*. Now that the *golden* or *silver goal* can terminate extra-time prematurely, *period* in fact turns out to be more apposite than *half*. More generally, teams can be said to enjoy or endure good or bad *periods* in a game, although ***spells*** is more common in this context.

Peripheral: We can identify two senses. One is on the way to becoming **anonymous**, as in 'Arsenal's **talisman** was *peripheral* against Bayern Munich'. The other amounts to a more scientific version of **awareness**, as in this appreciation by Sir Bobby Charlton of his uncle, Jackie Milburn: 'He must have had great *peripheral vision* because he always knew who was in the best shooting position – usually himself'. See **one thing on his mind**.

Philosophy: Those managers who speak foreign languages and wear glasses may be credited with a *philosophy* of their own. They might, for example, be known for an *attacking philosophy*, while their counterparts in tracksuits simply like to *get **bodies** into the box*. Arsène Wenger's professorial demeanour in particular has encouraged statements in the press that would not be out of place on an exam paper in Aesthetics: 'The idiosyncrasy of Wenger's *philosophy* is dissolved in the beauty of its effectiveness'. Discuss.

Pick: At most levels of football, players are *picked* and *dropped* for matches. But once they are good enough to feature in squads on the *international stage*, footballers are more likely to be *selected* and *omitted* – in fact the noun *omission*, coupled with the adjective *notable* or *most notable*, is usually privileged over the verb. As a rule the Anglo-Saxon monosyllables *pick* and *drop* evoke the rudimentary actions of a club manager; their Latinate equivalents, *select* and *omit*, are enlisted to suggest the more sophisticated **thoughts** of an international coach. Another example of the usefully hybrid nature of the English language is the availability of both *get stuck in* and *become involved* to describe a player's entrance into a **brawl**, depending on whether you want to be enthusiastic or euphemistic.

Pick and choose: 'He used to be a season-ticket holder, but he is *picking and choosing* his games these days'. An understated, but very barbed, criticism of a former *fanatic* who has become a *fair-weather fan* (having a wife and four children under the age of seven is not considered a sufficient excuse for turning up only when the *big boys* are in town). Football supporters are seldom praised by their own kind for showing any symptom of objective judgement.

Pick himself up: 'Lampard *picked himself up* and *coolly* despatched the penalty himself'. In those cases where the player who has earned the penalty happens to be the penalty-taker, reporters are careful to specify that he *picked himself up* (and maybe *dusted himself down* too) before doing so, just in case readers should think that he took the spot-kick while still prostrate in the box. Apart from themselves, footballers seem to *pick up* only three things in life (on the pitch at least): *knocks, runners* and *yellow cards*. For undisclosed technical reasons, it seems impossible to *pick up* a red card unless the referee drops it.

Pick his pocket: An expression where, for once, the defender, not the striker, is cast in the role of the thief: 'Baresi showed all his experience there and just *picked* the young man's *pocket*'. Used of players who **read** the game well and can nip in adroitly to take the ball off an attacker's foot with the minimum of fuss. The hapless forward, as well as being robbed, will find he gets *no **change*** out of Baresi ***all day*** long.

Pick out: In technical mode a reporter may find this verb useful to denote a *pinpoint* pass: 'Jan-Aage Fjortoft finished with ***aplomb*** after Moncur *picked*

him out brilliantly'. A commentator in hyperbolic
mode, after a ***screamer*** has just whistled in, may
exclaim, as if on behalf of the scorer: '*Pick* that one
out.' For the second usage, where a quick burst of ven-
triloquism interrupts the usual impartiality, compare
Welcome to the *Premiership*.

Pin up: No doubt *youth products* still get away
with pin-ups of the traditional variety in their corner
of the dressing room, but the one thing that you ritual-
istically *pin up* on its wall or door is criticism from
opponents or journalists. Sometimes a manager seems
as righteously indignant about the received wisdom
as Martin Luther nailing his 95 Articles to the church
door in Wittenberg: 'There's been so much rubbish
in the local press and the only motivation my ***lads***
needed today was the nonsense I *pinned up* to the
dressing-room door'. On other occasions, the ill-chosen
words are so current that drawing pins or blu-tac
are not required: 'I didn't do a *team-talk* – I just let
Mr Mellberg's comments *float* around the dressing
room'.

Pint-sized: The required footballing synonym for
small or ***diminutive*** when you want to find an idiom
that is instantly intelligible to the *average football
fan*.

Place: A synonym for *away ground*, usually laced
with respect: 'To come to *places* like Anfield is always
difficult'. A staple of post-match interviews, although
it would have been hard to predict twenty-five years
ago that the manager of Nottingham Forest would
ever say: 'Weymouth is a *tough place* to come and we
were under a lot of pressure'.

Play a bit: Understated validation of a good player,
seemingly always offered, complete with a little nudge,

by the elderly man sitting next to you: 'He can *play
a bit*'.

Play host: 'Everton *play host* to Wycombe Wanderers'.
An expression, like *entertain* ('Dagenham & Redbridge
entertain Ipswich') or **welcome**, in the thesaurus of
those who relay cup draws to avoid just saying *versus*
all the time, particularly on the occasion of the third
round of the FA Cup. The interchangeable verbs
thereby help to evoke the antiquity and gentility of
the competition, even if these courtesy terms are liable
to recede once the ceremony of the draw has been
completed, because one fan will simply say to another:
'We've *got* Southend away in the fourth round'. Since
the advent of multiple televised fixtures, the formali-
ties are rounded off by the elegant 'ties to be played
weekend *commencing*…'. Although it must be said that
the replacement of the traditional *bag* by the lottery-
inspired box has taken some of the *romance* out of the
occasion.

Playing surface: The *pitch*, when you wish to evaluate
its condition in more technical terms.

Play-off berth: Perhaps this image is used with the
hopeful implication that you may be travelling to a
higher division.

Plays his football: 'Mpenza, the Belgian international
who *plays his football* in Germany…'. The possessive
must always be used in this phrase in which the
embedded meaning involves 'work' rather than 'play'.

PLC: What a big publicly quoted football club gets
called when unpopular decisions driven by commer-
cial considerations are taken: 'No-one wanted me to
leave and I was happy at Sunderland, but the *PLC* had
to act'.

Pleasantries: Ironic description of an exchange between opposing players or *dugouts*: 'Phil Thompson swapped a few *pleasantries* with David O'Leary, who was left *fuming* after a two-footed tackle by Gerrard on Jlloyd Samuel'.

Pledge his future: Extravagantly quasi-matrimonial way of saying that a player is signing a new contract of some sort. 'Tomorrow, at a *hastily convened* press conference, he will be *pledging his future* to the Highbury *outfit*'.

Plum: Always used with *tie* to describe the most *mouthwatering fixture* of the round. It is most traditionally used, as if they are little Jack Horners, of lower-division teams who have pulled one of the *big boys* out of the hat. When there are still games to complete from the previous round, perhaps journalists are allowed an occasional mixed metaphor: 'Now Brentford have the carrot of the *plum draw* in the last eight dangling before them, should United beat Saints'. When a *heavyweight* **clash** is described as a *plum tie*, the fruit on offer is perhaps being viewed as much from the perspective of the television companies as the football clubs.

Plunder: A verb to indicate a keen appetite for goals, whether in a particular game – 'Twice in ten minutes Lampard *plundered* goals' – or in the course of a season – 'Nathan Ellington and Jason Roberts have *plundered* 25 goals between them'.

Poacher: Although clubs may *poach* a player (especially if Sir Alex Ferguson has **tapped** him **up** first), this word pertains chiefly to the activity of strikers. Thus a *gamekeeper turned poacher* describes the transformation of a defender into an attacker. The expression would not work so well the other way round (to refer to Dion Dublin, for example, instead of to Paul Warhurst). But it does fit well with the tendency in football to think of defenders and attackers as different species, the former steady and solid, the latter *lurking* and predatory. Criminal slang is on the side of the striker who *grabs* a goal or *snatches* a winner. Meanwhile, the poaching activity is reflected again in *brace*, used as a common synonym for 'two goals', and typically with the verb *bag* to complete the alliterative and metaphorical effect.

Point fingers: One of the classic phrases (compare *no disrespect to*) when a manager says he will not do something and then promptly proceeds to do it: 'I don't want to *point fingers* at any of my players but the defending on the third goal was *schoolboy stuff*'.

Poised: If a game is 1-1 or even 2-2 at half-time, summarisers tend to call the game *poised*, often *nicely* or *wonderfully* so. Whereas, when the early stages of a game have been *full of incident*, the game tends to have *all the makings* of an *absolute classic*.

Positives: In defeat, a consolation is to *take a lot of positives* from your *general play*, if you've given a *good account* of yourselves. The curious logic is that *positives* are not taken from a match when you have won it.

Posse: 'Immediately, referee Riley was *surrounded* by a *posse* of agitated Liverpool players'. Even before hip-hop, football used *posse* as the collective noun for a group of players *protesting* about a decision. We may also observe that the requisite verb for these situations is *surrounded*, even if there are only two people complaining. Alliteration also pushes *posse* forward when a group of clubs is *linked* to a player:

'A *posse* of Premiership clubs are currently contesting the Frenchman's signature'.

Possession: *Enjoyed* by the team who has it and sometimes more remarkable when it has not been *translated* into goals by the team *on top*. *Possession football*, in a set phrase, is played by a team that is passing fluently and **knocking** *it* **about**. 'Ball retention' is what rugby fans astray at a football match talk about.

Powder-puff: 'It was a *cup-final* game for us but we gave a *powder-puff* performance'. Ronnie Moore's exasperated description of his Rotherham team's showing in a relegation **six-pointer** provides an example of how *powder-puff* is a term where the innuendo after the hyphen can come into its own. *Tame* shooting attracts the same epithet: 'Tamworth's *efforts on goal* were largely of the *powder-puff* variety'.

Premiership: Introduced, disgracefully, as if there had been no **top-flight** football in England before the *money men* had their way. Statistical achievements are now that much easier to assert: 'Villa had not beaten Leicester in *Premiership* **history**'. A neologism lodged so successfully in football consciousness that we forget it has no pedigree. Imported from Scotland where the Premier Division had been formed in 1975-76 (perhaps in recollection of the Auld Alliance with France), it serves as a linguistic symptom of the inflation that has vitiated football now that it has become a business. The foundation of the *Premiership*, and the suggestion that you can be more first than first, dates from about the same time as starred As were first awarded in GCSEs. Grade inflation continues so that the *old* third division is now *League One*.

Preparation: The standard noun (generally in the singular) to be adopted in the run-up to any big game and particularly before an international tournament, it covers everything from results in recent friendlies to relationships within the *camp*, from penalty practice to the state of the hotel: 'Holland's *preparation* has been far from ideal, and the Saudis will fancy their chances of giving a good *account* of themselves'. It is also possible in these circumstances to exchange opinions and pass on rumours about a squad's *conditioning* if you want to sound more informed.

Pre-season: Often used as a virtual noun these days: 'Keane's *pre-season* was encouraging, which is bad news for the rest of the Premiership'.

Presence: Players can have *presence* in the theatrical sense (especially *in the **dressing room***) but much more common is the euphemism for strong tackling: 'Kamara is making his *presence felt* out there'. 'Kamara is *putting himself about*' is another way of putting it.

Pretty: As a rule used negatively in phrases justifying a pragmatic performance: 'Pilgrims boss Neil Thompson said: "It wasn't *pretty* but the points are vital"'. Even without the negative the adjective can still be disparaging, as in the phrase *pretty triangles*. See **ugly**.

Previous: A reduction, as in criminal slang, of *previous convictions*: 'Neill, who has *some previous* after his challenge on Carragher, made sure he took *all of* Bellamy there'.

Price tag: Clubs *place* one of these on **unsettled** players which they then *carry* until or even after they are sold. Serves also as a measure of the ***weight** of expectation* under which a record signing may buckle: 'Collymore *carried* such a big *price tag* into Anfield that he was never going to succeed there'. You can almost picture the *price tag* hanging round his neck, a numerical albatross. The image is well suited to the commoditisation of contemporary footballers, as they move from club to club. Similar in kind is the description of an international tournament as a *shop window* in which the participating players *showcase* their skills. Note also that when a lower-division chairman claims his ***starlet*** is *not for sale at any price*, this effectively marks the start of the bidding process, in the same way that his *vote of confidence* would be the beginning of the end for his manager.

Pride: What teams start *playing for* when well beaten, especially when their opponents are turning on the ***exhibition stuff***, or when they are playing a group game of only ***academic*** interest.

Problem: On the pitch, used of injuries – 'I think Ferguson has a bit of a *problem*, Clive' – or of the damage done by a fast or strong forward, frequently marked by a superlative phrase like *no end of, whole host of, all sorts of*: 'Salas is causing the England defence *all sorts of problems*'. Also a generic term for incidents in a player's private life: 'Merson's *off-the-field problems* have been ***well-documented***'. See ***selection headache*** for a *nice problem*.

Professional: Managers singing the praises of one of their players can go as far as to call him the *ultimate professional* or can settle for *consummate professional*, often adding for good measure that he displays a *very professional attitude* in training. During a game, anybody seen to be avoiding the ***cardinal sins*** is praised for *good professional play* (this encompasses the well-known *professional foul*). When the abbreviated form is used, it reflects the insider's perspective more sharply: 'We've got lots of good *honest pros* at this club'; 'He's developing into one of the *senior pros*'.

Progressive: Teams that favour a passing game tend to be praised for their *progressive football*. **Route One** teams are never criticised for 'regressive football' though.

Provider: This is what strikers become if they *lay on* a goal, but apparently only if they have scored first themselves: 'Proctor *turned provider* in the ninth minute when his cross was *met* by a Kevin Kyle *blockbuster*'. Should Kyle have *set up* Proctor previously, Proctor could be said to *return the compliment*. All these courtesies were more common before people became interested in *assists*.

Pub team: When a manager is laying into his players for **lacklustre** or amateur play, especially at their own end of the pitch, he often compares them to a Sunday morning *pub team*. The taunt casts the side as an irregular rabble, but there is also the implication that its players may be more interested in the piss-up after the game. Note an interesting variant from Neil Warnock bemoaning a bad piece of defending but not giving the attackers any credit either: 'It was an *alehouse* ball and someone not going with their man'. Other versions of this line in sarcasm include: 'You'll see better marking on *Hackney Marshes*' and 'My ten-year-old's *school team* concentrate better than our **back four**'. However, Ian Holloway's team-talks appear to have worked on at least one occasion: 'We were like the *Dog and Duck* in the first half and Real Madrid in the second'.

Pull on the shirt: A similar concept to stepping over the *white line*: 'When you *pull on that shirt*, you've got to be *completely focussed*'; 'When I *pulled on* the Scotland *shirt* I felt a real *buzz*'. Footballers must *pull* rather than 'put' on *shirts*, which have no buttons, but must not besmirch the *beautiful game* by *shirtpulling*.

Punch-up: *Almighty* or *ugly* are the usual qualifiers, and *brawl* or *bust-up* the preferred alternatives.

Pundit: In Hinduism, a holy man or teacher of wise sayings. In football parlance, a member of the *panel*, just as long as he can tell when his microphone is still running.

Punishment enough: The phrase employed when a player is sent off for a foul in the penalty area: 'Surely the award of the *spot kick* was *punishment enough*'. Can lead on to the complaint that the game has been *ruined as a spectacle*.

Purist: The unfortunate *purist* only ever makes an appearance at matches that are *not* for him or perhaps her. *Not for the purist* is always used to denote a high-scoring game. So whereas the *neutral* likes to see a *hatful* of goals, the *purist* seems to be a devotee of *tightness at the back*.

Purpose: *With purpose* is more common than 'purposefully' in football parlance: 'Zenden shot *with purpose*'; 'United have started this half *with real purpose*'. Sustained *purpose* amounts to *urgency*, but this quality is usually more conspicuous in football reporting by the *lack* of it, so *purpose* is often employed whenever people seem to be trying.

Put away: Primarily describes chances taken but also used with a bit more incisiveness (by analogy with boxing) of the opposition: 'Atletico looked out on their feet in the last fifteen minutes but we just couldn't *put them away*'.

Put through: A phrasal verb used to observe how forwards are ***released*** by a good pass, but never to describe the ensuing finish. The expression indicates a goal only when unfortunate defenders *put through* their own net.

Q

Quality: Increasingly common in singular adjective and noun form and, as in contemporary English more generally, always understood to be of *good quality*: 'It was a *quality* delivery'; 'Scholes's finish was *pure quality*'. In the plural, football people tend to be referring not so much to skill as tenacity or fortitude: 'We showed all our *battling qualities* out there in the second half'; 'Graham has tremendous *leadership qualities*'.

Queuing up to score: When the defence are caught undermanned as a cross is *whipped in*, the attacking team can be *mob-handed*: 'Look at that, Clive, there were three red ***shirts*** *queuing up to score*'. Queues of this kind seem rather slower to form for a penalty shoot-out.

Quiet: 'Orlygsson was having a *quiet* game out on the wing, ***completely*** *isolated* on the far touchline'. This does not mean Orlygsson wasn't shouting for the ball, but that he was making *no impression* on the match.

R

Raised hands: Everybody in the game seems to acknowledge that if you *raise your hands* you have only yourself to blame, regardless of what happens next, when the ref reaches for a ***straight*** *red*: 'I've no complaints about the sending off. Ricky Ravenhill *raised his hands* – he knows the rules and it's been ***dealt with***'.

Rap: Tabloid terminology for disciplinary proceedings: 'Blatter: Essien to face Hamann *rap*'.

Rattle the bar: Shots may *shave the post* or *remove paint* from the ***woodwork***, but the *bar*, when struck full on, tends to *rattle*. Sometimes both the strength of a shot and the speed of a subsequent event can be conflated for economy or dramatic effect: 'The bar *was still rattling* from Van Nistelrooy's penalty when referee Bennett blew the final whistle'.

React: Players on their mettle are *first to react*; if not they are *slow to react*, sometimes when it is not clear whether the ***situation*** necessitated reacting to anything. *Reaction* can commonly be an adjective describing a *save* or a noun standing in its place: 'Great *reaction* from Fox there'. It can also be used to describe the incidence of a recurring injury – 'Duncan suffered a *reaction* in training' – or a *hangover* effect – 'They clearly suffered a *reaction* from their great win at Hibs in the week'. More emphasis may be needed for an act of retaliation: 'It was a silly *over-reaction* from the ***lad***'.

Read: Pat Nevin was once spotted reading a book. He was henceforward known as *The Professor*. More commonly, it is the *game* itself that is *read*, usually by gnarled defenders or sagacious midfielders. *Reading the game well* means making good anticipatory decisions. Usually this literacy connotes experience – hence 'Rooney *reads the game* well for *one so young*' – or implies that the player in question is past his physical peak. The good *reader* may no longer be a good runner: 'McGrath *read* the ***danger*** brilliantly'.

Ready-made replacement: When a substitution is forced on a manager by injury and he has the luxury of making a ***straight*** *swap*, it is one of the rare moments in football where the stock phrase *in the **form** of* may justifiably be employed: 'Nigel fortunately has a *ready-made replacement, in the form of* Iwan Roberts, to bring on'.

Rearguard: A military term pressed into service when the wording of your report requires a variant: 'There was some stodgy defending by the Villa *rearguard*'. Otherwise used as an adjective to indicate a determined concentration on defence: 'Southampton adopted a *rearguard* action while Spurs threw caution to the wind'. 'Vanguard' is never used in football to refer to the attack.

Recognised: Football's own, rather polite way of saying 'proper' or 'full-time', this adjective should only be used in negative formulations: 'Spurs travel to the Priestfield without a *recognised* striker'; 'The Cobblers now have only one *recognised* centre-half on their books'. See also ***orthodox***.

Recognition: When *international **honours*** are bestowed on you and you win a ***full cap***, *recognition* has arrived. This is the economical way in which player profiles announce that a footballer has played for his country. Sometimes used in conjunction with the name of the national team in question – 'Bruce never earned England *recognition*' – though not apparently of those beyond the British Isles. Uncapped players talked up by programme notes may find themselves *on the edge of* or *not far off* international *recognition*.

Recruit: Describes a *recent **acquisition***, generally for a few months after he has been recruited. Often these days not qualified to play for England – 'Walsall's Portuguese *recruit*' – which means that *import,* or even the tautologous *foreign import*, may serve equally well.

Refuelling habits: The term *refuel,* perhaps at the risk of making these *habits* seem essential, conveys the finesse with which drinks will have been imbibed. This euphemism was apparently coined by Graham Taylor upon seeing a bar bill run up by two members of his England squad whose *off-pitch problems* have been **well documented**. It enjoys a continued existence even if foreign coaches, with their vaunted attention to *sports nutrition*, are doing their best to eliminate the *drinking culture* and drive kebab shops out of business.

Regular: As a noun preceded by *first-team*; as an adjective precedes ***first-team football***. Note also the reference to a team's *regular* strikers or keeper (used less of other positions). The phrase *on a regular basis* conveys the **week in week out** consistency to which all players and coaches aspire: 'Duff's always been quick and **tricky**, but now he's starting to score goals *on a regular basis*'; 'When I'm appearing in the team *on a more regular basis* then I will have *arrived*'. Use this longer phrase in preference to 'regularly' (in the same way as *at this moment in time* should be used rather than 'now', and *of late* instead of 'lately').

Regulation: Generally an indication of straightforward goalkeeping: 'It was a *regulation save*'; 'It came at *regulation height*'.

Reign: A managerial *spell* or period of *tenure* (though you seldom hear the latter) becomes a *reign* if at all successful or of any length (the two criteria tend to be linked), even though the reigns of English kings and queens could be both brutish and short: 'John Rudge's *reign* at Vale Park came to an end after 19 years'. Even the truest-blue scholar of football will hardly thank us for restating the following learned fact: 'Birmingham City did not win once in the *reign of* Pope John Paul I nor in the course of either of the conclaves before and after'.

Relax: What teams are sometimes asked to do in order to *express themselves*: 'In a funny way the first-leg deficit allowed us to *relax* and I told the players just to *go out and enjoy themselves*'. Off the pitch, since the abolition of the maximum wage, footballers admit to *relaxing* over *a meal and a glass of wine*, not a skinful of ale on an empty stomach.

Released: In an example of how commentary tends to praise **quality** *on the ball* ahead of **movement** off it, a perceptive pass is said to *release* the player it finds *into* **space**, even when the run made the pass possible. Otherwise *released* is the standard term for what happens to a player when his contract is terminated.

Relegation: A fruitful *zone* also for metaphor and melodramatic suggestion. Teams facing the *drop* find themselves in the *relegation zone*. Then, if results fail to improve, they find themselves *deep* in the *relegation mire*. They become *locked* in *relegation dogfights* and *scraps*. They are written off as *relegation fodder*. The *spectre* of *relegation looms* or *looks them in the eye*. They are *all but* down at the point when *survival* becomes only a *mathematical possibility*. In a final *coup de grâce*, they fall through the *relegation trapdoor*. *Finis*.

Representative: In the latter stages of knock-out tournaments, clubs or even countries find themselves increasingly described as *representative* of some larger entity to which they belong, particularly as other *representatives* fall by the wayside: 'Cameroon are Africa's only *representatives* left'; 'United, England's last remaining Champions League *representative…*'. This usage is not confined to football, but only in football can you read the following: 'FA Cup *surprise package* Farnham Town are alone in *flying the flag for* the Seagrave Haulage Combined Counties League'. See also *advert*.

Respect: It's extremely rare for managers whose teams have had a *wake-up call* to admit to having *underestimated* the opposition. Conversely, coaches of *underdogs* are more than happy to pronounce after a game that they gave the opposition *too much respect*. This may have taken the form of *standing off* and *letting them play*.

Respectable: 'That goal makes the *scoreline respectable*'. *Respectability* is a sort of *consolation*.

Restart: The beginning of the second half: 'Albion fell further behind within 35 seconds of the *restart*'. Tends not to be used, as might be supposed, when play resumes after a goal has been scored, nor when extra time begins.

Restraint: Because football is such a physical game, whenever there is *provocation*, any *restraint* shown by players is always *admirable* or *remarkable*: 'Dunfermline showed *admirable restraint* against FK

Vardar. The referee lives only 80 miles away from Skopje'.

Result: Without qualifying adjectives, *result* normally means *win*. Although the implication can be that *something* out of the game is better than nothing: 'Ibrox is a tough *place* to get a *result*'. When managers say 'it will be an achievement to get *any kind of result* at a *place* like this', they are probably not expecting *floodlight failure* before half-time but implying that their team will get beaten. *Results elsewhere* are what worried benches and fans keep their eye on late in the season, especially if their fate is *out of their hands*. These fans may include *old boys*. 'I always look for their *result* first' is the standard, incontrovertible proof of a player's undying loyalty to the club he has left for a richer one. He may indeed still have *lots of friends* at his former club, even if he prefers the *set-up* at his new one.

Resurrect: Teams can be *crucified* (sometimes *absolutely crucified*) when defeated humiliatingly, but *resurrect* is normally used when an individual player has an opportunity to *kick-start* his fortunes: 'Transfer-listed Geoff Horsfield let two *golden* chances to *resurrect* his City career go begging'.

Return: Destined to be *emotional* if a player or manager coming back to his former club remains on good terms with it (or if Kevin Keegan is involved at all). To be contrasted with *warm welcome*.

Revel: Players or teams can be said to *revel in the conditions*: 'Terry Phelan really seems to be *revelling* in this searing heat in Orlando'. Individual players may also *revel* in an *unfamiliar role*.

Revolving door: Clubs with a rapid turnover in managers are imagined as having one of these: 'There's been a *revolving door* at Blundell Park for the last few years and this *football club* needs some stability'. Some managers, you can imagine, never really get out of the door, let alone into the *hot seat*.

Reward: A goal when scored by a hard-working striker: 'Gary Lund got his *reward* on 75 minutes'. A goal is in general only a *reward* when it is the first or only goal the rewarded player scores. No player, it seems, deserves a *reward* of more than one goal.

Rifle: The first-choice verb for recording the precision and speed of the expert *marksman*: 'Masanga *rifled* a first-time volley past Scott Carson'. *Drill* comes a close second and the focal action is much the same: 'Andy Liddell *drilled in* an angled free-kick'. There are other alternatives to give us a momentary sense of the line of flight or the point of impact: 'O'Shea *speared* a shot into the top corner'; 'Kenny Miller *arrowed* home a second'. But the essential aim with all these verbs is to telescope the event: 'Sam Bangoura was on hand to *rifle* a corner of the net'.

Right: Perhaps the classic footballing example occurs when a commentator is enthusing about an exceptional piece of play: 'What a goal! Van Basten had *no right* to score from there'. He of course means to appreciate rather than to invalidate the goal. But when the *right* you do not have becomes *divine*, it always features in admonitory phrases, often warning against complacency of different kinds: 'Forest know that no club has a *divine right* to be playing *top-flight* football'. Meanwhile, when referees or linesmen are commended by the studio panel or commentators – it has been known to happen – the officials are these days said to *get it right* rather than simply to 'be right'.

Right spirit: Reporters will, as though on the **neutral**'s behalf, sometimes comment approvingly at the end of a match that it was *played* in the *right spirit*. No less specific yet as undefined as the *right spirit* are the *right reasons* for talking about a match or perhaps a player, notably when there have been problems hitherto: 'After that display, Manish, we can talk again about Rooney *for all the right reasons*'.

Rightly so: A headmasterish afterthought after disciplinary procedures: 'Simeone has been booked for that display of petulance and *rightly so*'. 'He can have *no complaints* about that', summarisers will sometimes echo. The moralising voice may become strident, as in this prediction by an England fan recorded in a broadsheet: 'Alpay will be lynched when he gets back to England – and *rightly so*'.

Rise: Perhaps to indicate how easily they have **latched onto** a cross in comparison to a *backpedalling* defender, forwards are said to *rise*, rather than **climb** (that means something else), often *unchallenged*, at the far post for a floated or hanging cross.

Roar: Noun used to describe the orchestrated encouragement of the crowd, but perhaps less common nowadays. The *Roker Roar* is no longer; the *Hampden Roar* has been muted by all-seater reform.

Roast: The verb suggests, among other possibilities, that a full-back is feeling the heat because of a winger's *searing* pace, and that he is being *turned* continuously as if on a spit. Some defenders become so discombobulated by *chasing shadows* that they can be said to have contracted *twisted blood*.

Rocket: Occasionally a synonym for **screamer**, but more usually employed as a metaphor for motivational team talks: 'Ian Porterfield seems to have given his players a *real rocket* at half-time'. When referring to individual mentoring, the metaphor becomes even more vivid: 'Darren was *off the pace* earlier in the season, and we had to *put a rocket up him* a few times to get his attitude right'.

Role: 'He's been given a *free role* behind the front two'; 'He has a *roving role* in the midfield'. Sometimes a *role* seems to come with an official permit: 'McManaman's got a *licence* to wander'. The term tends to imply an element of creativity, whereas man-marking, for example, is often just a *job*. When they **hang up** their *boots*, ageing old *pros* may be promised they *still have a role to play at the club* (not merely as lottery-ticket sellers these days, but under the guise of hospitality).

Roll: The cool way these days to take a penalty, as opposed to **blasting** it from the spot, but the cool way puts a higher premium on the keeper *guessing* wrong: 'The Duke calmly *rolled* his penalty down the centre as Davis obligingly dived to his left'.

Roof: *Nets* and *grounds* are the two places in football where you tend to notice the *roof*. The *roof* can *come off* the latter if the ball *hits the roof* of the former. The metaphor still works even when all four sides of the ground you're commentating at are uncovered. Note also the verb form for an *emphatic* finish: 'Aizlewood **gleefully** *roofed* that one from five yards out'.

Room: In football, this is more often a verb than a noun, employed when players away in Europe or on *international* **duty** share a hotel room – curiously, even the richest football clubs like to economise in this way with the premise of building team morale. It has become the standard form by which a footballer indicates, without undue sentimentality, that a particular team-mate is also his best mate. 'I always *room* with Smithy'.

Rooted: Applicable when the goalkeeper makes no move at all, with *to the spot* left understood: 'Zico's free kick left Alan Rough *rooted*'.

Rotation: Has a scientific sound to it, especially when paired with *policy* or *system*: 'Chelsea operate a *squad rotation system* and Hernan will have to get used to that'. But the related verb, when conjugated, encourages less professional-sounding alternatives: 'I *rotate*, you *tinker*, he *chops and changes*'. There was, in the days of the German Democratic Republic, a club called *Rotation Berlin*, but it was no doubt the team of a propeller works or a tank-turret factory.

Round ball: Plenty of sports use a round ball, but football is usually understood to be *the* definitive *round ball game*, when you're contrasting it with the *oval ball game* and, say, moving rapidly between rugby and football results. *Ball* is the standard word in the general run of play, whereas *football* can suggest a more special kind of relationship: 'You've got to treat that *football* like a friend'; 'The things Cruyff could do with a *football* had to be seen to be believed'. See also **matchball**.

Round off: A goal which concludes a nice **passage** *of play* or a *neat interchange* of passes, is generally said to *round off the move*. *Move*, usually a composite of several passes, should not be confused with **movement**.

Round up: 'Eleanor will now *round up* the rest of the Scottish results'. To the uninitiated, it may sound as though Eleanor will be adding a goal here or there to the totals, but it's a way of summarising the results, once they have, of course, been *classified*.

Route One: The favoured itinerary of the *long-ball merchants*. Pejorative in most cases: 'They're just a *Route One*, *hit-and-hope* team'. The phrase has been ascribed to the 1970s television programme *Quiz Ball*, where footballers who fancied their general knowledge could score either by answering one hard question (*Route One*) or by putting together answers to several easier questions ('route four' has never caught on to describe *inter-passing*). *Playing catch-up*, now popular to describe a team *chasing* a particular *game* or pursuing league leaders in the title *run-in*, is a phrase which sounds American but may owe its introduction into football language to that most European of quiz shows, *Going for Gold*.

Roy of the Rovers: For extra emphasis and alliteration, usually *real Roy of the Rovers stuff*, after the football comic serialisation set in Melchester, as near to 'Manchester' as you can get without alienating Merseyside readers. Chiefly used when a *youth product* makes his mark early in his career, often for his *home-town club* (although you may remember Roy Race was not actually born in Melchester). Roy Hodgson's brief managerial *reign* at Blackburn provoked some new, largely unjustified uses of the phrase. Other references to cartoon characters, also rather obsolescent now, are *Billy Whizz* and *Captain Marvel*. The names of individual players likewise give sub-editors some scope for fairly gratuitous headlines: '*Flash Gordon* fires Canaries towards Europe'; '*Dennis the Menace* breaks Scottish *hearts*'.

Ruined as a spectacle: Tends to be used in postmortems to games where there has been an early

sending-off: 'Referee Mike Dean followed the letter of
the law but it *ruined* the game *as a spectacle*'.

Rule out: What injuries do to players: 'Owen's hamstring *rules him out* of the midweek **clash**'. Tempting
as it is to picture the hamstring getting a ruler out and
putting a line through Owen's name, the usage is so
automatic as to be invisible.

Run of play: Locution which necessitates the preposition *against*, used exclusively when a team
scores though being outplayed. We thereby infer that
an **injustice** has occurred. On local radio, perhaps
understandably, the non-regional team always seems
to score *very much against the run of play*.

Run riot: Though threatening at times to be interpreted literally since the advent of **hooliganism**, still
used figuratively to denote the superiority of one
team.

Run the clock down: Opposing teams *waste time* or,
more idiomatically and bookably, are guilty of *timewasting*. But your own players would never do that.
They merely *run the clock down*. The adjective for
them is **cynical**; the adjective for you is **professional**.

Run-in: 'Of the contenders, Arsenal have the trickier
run-in'. Refers to the fixtures towards and at the end
of the season which decide championship, promotion
and relegation *issues*. No-one knows exactly when a
run-in starts.

Running: Like classy racehorses, good teams and
players are always *full* of it.

Rush of blood: Although this term is interchangeable with *moment of madness* for players who *raise*

their hands or suddenly launch into a *two-footed challenge*, it is reserved in particular for keepers who charge out of their area (admittedly in a *rush*) only to find themselves in **no man's land**: 'After Weaver's **rush of blood**, City found themselves down to ten men'. Sometimes unfair in that the only option would have been an attempt to ***improvise a clearance***.

S

Sack of spuds: Used so frequently in similes to describe a player *going to ground* too *easily* that it has become *proverbial*, as indeed have sacks containing less edifying material: 'Nobby Solano just tried to *brush off* his challenger, who went down like the *proverbial sack of wotsisname*'. Players blessed with pace can also prove as quick as wotsisname *off a shovel*.

Sacrifice: Teams *reduced* to *ten men*, by the loss of a defender or a goalkeeper in particular, need to be *reorganised* rapidly. To this end a player, usually a striker or a midfielder, is invariably *sacrificed*. Hyperbolic as the verb may be, it does make clear that the substitution has been forced on both player and manager: 'Spare a thought for striker Louis Soares, the man *sacrificed* for the **introduction** of Flitney's replacement Scott Tynan'.

Salmon: 'Tony Dennis leapt like a *salmon* for such a small man and Taylor *applied* the finishing touch'. The simile is always reserved for headers where the player has *got up well*, often when he is **pint-sized**. Goalkeepers do not leap in this way, since they are already supposed to be like **cats**.

Saw it all the way: Another circumlocution (always to be used in this tense) to indicate that a goal-keeper made a routine save: 'It was not a bad *effort* from Jim Tolmie, but Avramovic *saw it all the way*'. Conversely, if the keeper *never saw it*, it was assuredly a great goal.

Scalp: *Scalps* are taken in the Cup by *giant-killing* teams. The metaphors are consistent with one another even if they add up to being a conflation of Native American history and biblical narrative. Scalps in football are usually *notable,* occasionally *prized.*

Scandinavian: 'The ball fell at Pedersen's feet and the *Scandinavian* needed *no second invitation* to *slot* it *home*'. Live commentators will remind you where a player is from instead of repeating the name again and again. For some reason, Norwegians, Danes, Swedes and Icelanders, of which there are many in British football, often seem to get called *Scandinavian* players, while Spaniards are not called 'Iberians' or Croatians 'Slavs'. This is probably because the commentators are not exactly sure where Pedersen comes from. *South American* is also useful in case you confuse Bolivia and Venezuela, but Brazilians are more frequently identified as 'Brazilians' than 'South Americans'. Another reason for the hold-all terms may be that they convey certain archetypal character-istics: reliability and steadiness in the case of the Scandinavians as opposed to skill and mischief with the South Americans. The periphrasis is thus likely to surface in place of the player's name when the stereotype is active: 'It was a *glaring* miss from Solano after the *South American* had brilliantly *jinked* his way into the danger zone'.

Scenes: *Fantastic scenes* is how hyped-up commenta-tors remark on a jubilant crowd exulting in their team's victory. *Disgraceful scenes* is the corresponding phrase when **hooliganism** *rears its ugly head*.

Schoolboy: A standard qualifier for *error* and *defending*. Despite the origins of the term (see **howler**), it tends to mean *abject* rather than particularly **naive**.

Scoop: Aptly describes what happens when a striker gets underneath the ball from close in: 'Seol *fashioned* the miss of the match as he *scooped* his shot over from six yards'. The effect is more extravagant in 'the ball was *ladled* into the stand by Teemu Tainio'.

Scoreline: Commonly teamed with *reflection* and *play*, particularly when England are losing: 'The *scoreline* is not a true *reflection* of the *play*'. *Score* would seem perfectly serviceable, but *scoreline* is often preferred by journalists allergic to monosyllables.

Scrappy: Often when there is no **shape** to either team or *pattern* to the game, it will be described as a *scrappy* **affair**. A *scrappy* goal (but *they all count*) never *lives long in the memory*, or, if you like the kind of extravagant understatement which is so popular in football parlance, 'it won't be winning any **goal of the season** *awards*'.

Scraps: What *predatory* strikers *starved* of **service** are reduced to feeding off: 'Austria's *well-marshalled* defence left Armstrong and Hamilton with only a few *scraps*'. Perhaps this is why forwards appear so greedy when an opportunity does arise: 'Malcolm Christie *gobbled up* the *rebound*'; 'Robert Pires *devoured* the half-chance'.

Screamer: A shot that results in a goal, often qualified as an *absolute screamer*. Presumably derived from the sound that the *howitzer* makes through the air as it flies towards goal. It has been known for commentators, perhaps when they want to emphasise the richness of the **contact**, to drop the 's': 'An absolute *creamer* from Tony Currie there'.

Scuff: Almost the regular term for missing from close range: 'There were two *decent* chances *scuffed* by Darren Huckerby'. The verb can also indicate a goal with a *miscued* shot – 'Kezman *stole in* to *scuff* the ball into the net' – and be applied more generally for an unimpressive team performance – 'Hoddle's new charges *scuffed* their way to a draw'.

Scythe: The orthodox implement for a primitive tackle: 'Fernando Hierro was fortunate to escape a red card when he *scythed* Dyer to the turf in the forty-ninth minute'. Lumberjacks may also be hired and fired: 'Van Persie was shown the red card for his *intemperate felling* of Le Saux'. Maybe more sophisticated equipment gives the tackler more margin of error: 'A *combine harvester* of a tackle by Danny Mills had the manager leaping out in approval'.

Sea of players: Emphasises a particularly dense *crowd scene*: 'Scholes's shot went through a *sea of players*, hit the far upright and bounced away'. Particularly generous defences have been known to *part like the Red Sea*. A **coach and horses** may then be in order.

Second ball: You must not hit the **first man**, but you must win the *second ball*. As with **fifty-fifties** (which they sometimes become), the outcome of *second balls* is remembered by managers to illustrate commitment to the **cause**.

See: 'Le Tissier *saw* his penalty saved by Crossley'; 'Barry *saw* his goalbound header *cleared off the line* by Kelly'. A little trick of journalistic narrative through which the reporter seems momentarily to collude with the player denied. There is probably no guarantee that the player actually had time to *see* the unsuccessful outcome. If a player beats his man with some skill and impudence, one or two summarisers will on his behalf address the hapless opponent with the mischievous words *see you later*.

See red: In standard English, the phrase for a momentary loss of control. In football, particularly in hurried evening editions or compressed Ceefax prose, the term stretches to embrace not only what happens to players who lose their tempers but what happens to them once the referee loses patience: 'Mikkel Beck *saw red* after his reckless tackle'. A reliteralised idiom, in effect.

Seemingly: Adopted, sometimes with the effect of splitting an infinitive, when hindsight tells you there was a subsequent turnaround in a game: 'Sunderland got two more, from Proctor and Phillips, to *seemingly* put the tie beyond Souness's **men**'.

Seen those given: In the immediate aftermath of a referee *waving away* appeals for a spot-kick, the summariser will study the replay and use this phrase if he thinks that a case can be made for the prosecution, even if he agrees with the official that it was not a *nailed-on* penalty: 'It was questionable whether Knight did take the man but I've *seen those given*, Martin'.

Selection headache: Managers with a full complement of players or an *array of talent* at their disposal, traditionally suffer from this ailment. This kind of *headache* is 'a *nice* **problem** to have'. But resist any inclination to *tinker*.

Sell-by date: 'Several players in the Blackpool line-up seem to have reached their *sell-by date*'. This usage has probably become more common since refrigeration and supermarkets, but – especially after **Bosman** – players really do have a *sell-by date* in that clubs are anxious to *ship* them *on* with time left on their contracts in order to *recoup* something of the original fee. There is a celebrated example where Gordon Strachan did not seem to fancy his chances of reducing to clear: 'I've got a yoghurt to finish by today, the expiry date is today. That can be my priority rather than Agustin Delgado'. The less polite trade terms for players who are past their best include *washed up, gone* and *shot*.

Sell short: Underhit passes, particularly backpasses now that keepers have to kick them, warrant this verb: 'The backpass from Beckham *sold* James *well short* but he *spread himself* well'. The usage is comparable with doing one of your team-mates no **favours** or, in a more ironic version, of *rather overestimating his athletic abilities*.

Send the keeper: 'Marlon Harewood was coolness personified as he ran up and *sent the keeper* the wrong way.' Always implicit here is the fact that the penalty-taker has scored from the spot, whether he has *given* the goalkeeper *the eyes* or not. From the opposite point of view, even though it is possible for a keeper to *guess right* and only **get a hand to** a penalty, the fact that he has dived in the right direction is more worthy of note if he pulls off a save: 'Paul Cooper *guessed right* again and Ipswich breathed a sigh of relief'.

Servant: Usually in the expression *great servant to the club*. It is impossible to have been a *great servant* for a short period of time. *Great servants* have to be loyal and preferably a bit unspectacular: 'Jason Dodd has been a *great servant* to Southampton'. Tony Adams, on the other hand, though he could be called a *great servant* by most criteria, is **afforded** *legendary status* for being that bit better. To be an **ambassador**, there usually has to be an element of international *duty*.

Service: Provided by the midfield to the forwards. *Misfiring* strikers are excused when deprived of it: 'Jardel and Grabbi are not to blame. They're getting no *service*'. *Normal service* is resumed when a striker rediscovers his scoring *touch* or a team recovers its form. In the plural, a somewhat archaic way of announcing a purchase: 'We're very pleased to have secured Carl's *services*'. Motorway *service stations*, incidentally, only get mentioned in football when the *tiny minority* of **so-called fans** arrives or if there are *bungs* to be administered by a manager who may on these occasions bring a briefcase rather than a **chequebook**.

Set piece: A *dead-ball* **situation**, whether a free kick or corner (from some players a *long throw* is *as good as a corner*), at which a team can exploit a carefully prepared manoeuvre: 'We've been working on *set pieces* all week'. Sometimes it would seem that all the practice put in on the **training ground** can work to the detriment of the team's all-round play: 'England have only threatened from *set pieces*'.

Settle: May occur in several footballing contexts. Players can *fail to settle* at a new club, usually because their wives do not like Birmingham or on account of language difficulties. When, say after 70 minutes, a team is said to be *settling for a draw*, this is a dignified way of saying that they're not exactly trying their hardest. Whereas an early goal can *settle* the nerves, a late strike will *settle* the contest: '**Honours** were even until Kuqi *settled it* in their favour'.

Set up: There is an increasingly common verbal usage to describe a manager's choice of formation for difficult assignments, perhaps influenced by the way in which technical directors of Formula One teams *set up* their cars depending upon track conditions: 'When Curbishley *strings* five across midfield, the Addicks are *set up* beautifully to counter attack in away games'; 'Burnley *set* themselves *up* well, looked for that one opportunity and they took it when it came'. This variant from Walter Smith has vestiges of the **stall** about it: 'We've had a lot of games where we've been able to *set* ourselves *out* defensively'.

Set-up: A euphemism beloved of new signings when a move earns them a large wage increase, it is supposed to mean the ground, facilities and much else at a club: 'I was just so impressed by the *set-up* at Middlesbrough that I didn't hesitate to put pen to paper'. In its most expansive version, when *facilities* are *second to none*, a recent **acquisition** can praise *the whole set-up from the chairman down to the tea-lady*. Not that there is likely to be a tea-lady these days.

Shape: A polyvalent word which can apply to the team, the act of shooting or the shot itself. *Shape* is *kept* by good teams and *lost* by disorganised ones: 'I like the *shape* of the team today with the wing backs pushing up to support'. You can describe the act of someone getting his body into a good position to shoot with a reflexive verb: 'Rae controlled the ball, *shaped himself* and hit an *unstoppable* 30-yard volley past Jasskeläinen'. Meanwhile, the alliterative phrase *shape to shoot* describes the act of feigning a shot: 'Jevons *shaped to shoot* but instead passed low into the penalty area'. In a usage perhaps borrowed from golf, *curled* **efforts** are often described as having *great shape to* or *on* them.

Shepherd: Although *shepherds* – at least in the *One Man and his Dog* version – spend all their time getting sheep *into* pens, in football the phrase is used exclusively for the action whereby a defender *shepherds* the ball *out* of play, usually managing to **block** *off* an attacker in the process.

Ship goals: When defences are *all at sea*, they are always likely to *ship goals*. *Leak goals* is a close cousin. Broadsheet writers are allowed to refer to *porous* defences.

Shirt: Although **socks** and shorts are no less distinguishing, this is the favoured metonym: 'Today sees Kilcline's 250th appearance in a Sky Blue *shirt*'. In the plural used to indicate the number of players gathering in offensive or defensive positions: 'Serbia have got plenty of blue *shirts* into the **mix** for this free kick'; 'There are plenty of red *shirts* behind the ball here'.

Shoot on sight: A phrase which once summarised the policy designed to thwart break-outs from Colditz or escape over the Berlin Wall, and which now designates the conduct of players who think the keeper is **dodgy**, or who enjoy the **luxury** of a lead: 'With a two-goal **cushion** the Hornets started to adopt a *shoot-on-sight policy* and Devlin, Mahon and Fitzgerald all attempted *long-range* **efforts** that failed to *trouble* Banks'.

Shoot ourselves in the foot: 'We keep *shooting ourselves in the foot* at set pieces'; 'We *shot ourselves in the foot* at both ends of the pitch'. A purely verbal ritual engaged in by managers who may feel like shooting themselves, or their players, in other parts of the **anatomy**.

Shooting boots: The index of a striker's form. He can *seem to have lost* them, then he *finds* them, then he *really finds* them. But he certainly needs to *remember* them in the first place: 'Reading might have won comfortably had on-loan striker Lloyd Owusu *remembered* to *put on* his *shooting boots*'. There do not seem to be 'tackling' or 'passing' boots; rather a defender or midfielder may be said to *recapture his form*, to be *back to his best* or *like his old self*.

Shore up: Defences can be *bolstered* at the start of a match (by a player returning after an injury lay-off) and *shored up* in the course of a game (thanks to a substitution).

Shotstopper: Synonym for goalkeeper which emphasises a particular facet of his game (being *good on his line*), usually at the expense of other attributes he might be expected to have. The noun generally crops up in an affirmative phrase which is then quickly qualified: 'Rhys Wilmot has always been a great *shotstopper*, but he does not **command** his area at all and his *kicking* is *woeful*'.

Shoulder: *Old-fashioned* shoulder *charges* or *barges* are less frequently sighted (or cited) these days. But good *predatory* strikers are always *on the shoulder* of the **last man**. Those nostalgic for **wingers** who had more *guile* and less **pace** than their modern counterparts like to remember how they would *drop their shoulder*, before swaying their hips with a *bodyswerve*.

Shout: Players faced with a decision whether to play the ball often *need a shout* from one of their team-mates: 'That's a **soft** corner. Hyypia just *needed a shout* from Dudek there'. Such is the cosmopolitan nature of the modern-day Premiership that these lapses are often ascribed to a *breakdown in communication*. *Shout* is also a synonym for *appeal* in the context of penalties.

Show: Often used with the adjective *late*, sometimes, for devotees of Noel Edmonds or Gaye Byrne, with the adjective doubled up: 'United's *late late show*'. Teams or their star players can be *late to show*, by analogy with racehorses, meaning that it was only towards the end that *class* told: 'A *late show* from Raúl gave Madrid the points'. A player who *shows too much* to an opponent yields possession carelessly to him, while a goalkeeper can also be guilty of committing himself too early: 'Lee Grant *showed* far *too much* of his inside left post as the resulting shot was *squeezed* past him'.

Showboating: To play to the gallery. Like *ballwatching*, always one of the *cardinal sins* that footballers may commit. Scorned as *unprofessional* whenever and wherever it is seen.

Shudder: The choicest verb to render the impact, as well as something of the sound, of the ball against the *woodwork*: 'Rooney unleashed a *thunderous effort* from 30 yards that *shuddered* Blackburn's furthest post'. Sometimes the rhythm of the game will suggest particular alternatives: 'Idiakez also *rattled* a post and *shivered* the bar in the second half'. *Shuddering* is also available for selection along with *crunching* for a tackle which takes *man and ball*.

Sidelined: Synonym for *injured* but often with the implication that the player will be *out* for the *foreseeable future* or the rest of the season. Such a player will always be described as *on* and not, as one might expect, 'behind' the *sidelines*.

Siege: When *one-way traffic* gets held up by a stalwart goalkeeper or by a particularly resolute defence, the metaphor shifts and football becomes a war again – the goal is *under siege* by the team *encamped* in the opponent's half. Managers who see their teams regularly *under siege* are subject to a different version of the same metaphor: '*Beleaguered* Glenn Roeder saw West Ham throw away their lead'.

Signing: Noun synonymous with, but more common than, *purchase* or **acquisition** or *buy* or **recruit**. Although players who have **come through** the ranks and been at one club all their career will also have had plenty of contracts to sign (from *schoolboy forms* to that final one-year *extension*), *signings* must have come from another club. Indeed, their provenance is often mentioned in the same breath: 'Spurs' Ukrainian *signing* will need some time to *adjust*'; 'The inspired *signing* from Partick *bagged* yet another *brace*'. Sometimes the literal meaning is rendered more visible when, at the risk of sounding like an autograph-hunter, a manager declares himself pleased to have *secured* a player's *signature*, or when a player agrees to *sign on the dotted line* for the interested club, a moment which will be captured for posterity at a *hastily convened* press conference.

Silence: So often the *silence* of home fans when their team concedes is *stunned*. Partisan commentators can also describe such silences as *deafening*, with the same kind of ironic intent as those strikers who **wheel away** to *cup their ear* to the home fans.

Silverware: A synonym for *trophies*, often uttered by players who are lucky enough to have signed for a club with **ambition** while remaining conscious of the dangers of presumptuousness: 'I wanted the chance of some *silverware*. And Celtic have given me that'.

Some managers can be intimidated by *senior pros* who are fully paid-up members of the *show-us-your-medals* **brigade**, but Martin Jol is clearly impressed with the **honours** bestowed on Edgar Davids: 'He is maybe the biggest player in England, if you think about his *silverware*'.

Sink in: Promotion is an achievement which, as a rule, *sinks in* only on the day that the **computer** produces the fixture list for the following season (complete with **big boys**). As in other sports, a triumph of any moment does not *sink in* as long as you are actually using that verbal phrase. Phrases like 'It's yet to *sink in*, Gary' or 'It just hasn't *sunk in* yet, Garth' are a way of fending off tiresome interviewers who want your thoughts while the rest of the **lads** are celebrating. By the time a victory does *sink in*, the player has moved on to different vocabulary: 'Obviously it was nice to win the Cup, but we've got to *look forward* now'.

Sit: What *anchoring* or *holding* players do in front of the **back four**. As the position of the man who *protects* the defence and allows other midfielders to *play* has become more specialised, so a number of terms to describe it have evolved: 'Whatever the formation of the midfield, Makelele is the *sitter*'; 'Amady Faye, *parked* in front of the defence, has been equally influential as a *screen*'. A last example gets carried away by its wordplay, but again provides evidence of how important the position is, and of how peerless the Chelsea number four is considered to be: 'Butt plays as the *buttress* in front of the **back four** in the role that is now known as the *Makelele*'.

Sit up: The verb *sit up* refers to the preferred behaviour of the ball as a striker prepares to hit it: 'Although Akinbiyi was in **yards** of **space**, it just would not *sit up* for him'. It is equally frustrating if a bouncing pass will not *sit down* so that a striker can get *over the top* of it. But there are occasions when the ball can be more co-operative: 'For the crucial goal, it just *sat up* and *winked* at me'.

Sitter: The classic cliché for a very easy chance, usually combined with *absolute* or *complete* and usually missed. Presumably the underlying reference is to the proverbial 'sitting duck'. The word appears first to have been used in cricket around the turn of the century to denote easy catches, but in football it is reserved for errors by strikers, never goalkeepers.

Situation: Football is just full of *situations* – *deadball situations*, *dropball situations*, *play-off situations*, *must-win situations*, *unsavoury situations*. The term has prospered to the point of featuring redundantly in some commentaries: 'If Rovers can win this one game, they'll be in a *semi-final situation*'.

Sixes and sevens: Not an expression unique to football (it comes from City of London Livery Companies squabbling over their place in the Lord Mayor's parade), but used specifically in the game for defences in disarray: 'The Blackburn defence was at *sixes and sevens* again on the half-hour *mark*.'

Sixpence: Still defying decimalisation, the little *sixpence* serves to show either how neatly a player can turn or how accurately he can place a pass: 'Cassells *turned on a sixpence*, beat two men and found the top corner'; 'Armstrong *put it on a sixpence* right into Holmes's path'.

Six-pointer: Seamlessly upgraded in the English game (although Arthur Cox sometimes forgets) from its antecedent *four-pointer*. As if further exaggeration were needed, the phrase is usually amplified: '***Make no mistake***, this is a *real six-pointer* if ever there was one'.

Skin: What wingers do to full backs when they are giving them a ***torrid time*** or letting them know they have been *in a game*: 'Russell *skinned* his defender before *slotting* home'. Similar culinary metaphors involve being *done like a kipper* or ***roasted***.

Sky-high: One of those hyphenated phrases *ever-present* in football (compare ***kick-start***, ***new-look***). Like its opposite *rock-bottom*, used to qualify confidence: 'After the three back-to-back wins, confidence in the *camp* is *sky-high* at the moment'.

Sleep: 'Tottenham *went to sleep* once again *at the back*'. In this example *at the back* seems like a place conducive to rest, as in the cinema or a classroom. Defences can also get *caught napping,* most likely by a quickly taken free kick.

Sleeping giant: Denotes a big, once successful club now dormant in the lower divisions. This *giant* must be a deep sleeper, spending several years out of the ***top flight***, *languishing* in the lower divisions (Wolves, say, in the 1980s and 1990s), before earning the accolade. The image is not applicable on the *international stage* where sluggish nations, pre-eminently Spain, should be described as *perennial underachievers*.

Slick: Can be used as an adjective for a good passing surface, as a verb in the same context – 'rain has *slicked* the ***top***' – or to describe the passing skills of a side who are so good it looks as if rain has *slicked* the surface every week: 'Depor's *slick* passing has to be seen to be believed.'

Slide rule: An adjectival phrase applied to admirably precise, *measured* or weighted passes. For another example of defunct technology in football, see *carbon copy*.

Slightest of touches: A superlative called much into action during commentaries: 'The *slightest of touches* took it past the keeper'. Uttered when, for instance, a *glancing header* finds the net, a *cruel **deflection*** wrongfoots the stopper, or a player connects with a cross that has been *whipped in* at pace. When such a *ball in* narrowly fails to be converted, we hear that it *needed* only *the slightest of touches*.

Sloping pitch: 'Cradley Town boss Trevor Thomas believes levelling the *infamous sloping pitch* at Beeches View will stop players turning their noses up at the club'. If a pitch has a *slope* it always seems to be *famous* or *infamous*, even though there have been countless examples in the lower reaches over the years where such a pitch has proved a *great leveller* in the cup.

Slump: Provided that they are already at the *wrong end* of the table, teams seem to *slump to defeats*, especially if they are *successive*. The verb hints at some general inertia about the club, beyond the particular match in question. These days it seems you need to lose only three times in a row for *parachute payments* to be anticipated: 'After a nightmare November, Charlton are a club *in freefall*'.

Smart: Tends to be used of saves which are as a rule more difficult than ***regulation*** but which the keeper is nevertheless expected to make: 'Keelan had to ***react*** smartly to keep out a David Johnson header'. Managers are always wary of facing teams *smarting* from a recent defeat, with *a point to prove*.

Smash-and-grab raid: 'Table-topping Norwich *crashed* to their first defeat in eight games – the victims of a Cardiff *smash-and-grab raid*'; '*Former* Watford striker Tommy Smith *dented* Reading's promotion hopes in a Derby *smash-and-grab* at the Madjeski'. The most contemporary version of a time-honoured truism that teams who soak up pressure and hit the opposition successfully on the break have *nicked* the points or *mugged* the other team. A way of suggesting that *highway* or *daylight robbery* can occur, even *under the lights*.

Smoking cigars: 'Their goalkeeper never had a *sweat on* and their two centre-halves were *smoking cigars*. It was *Sunday-morning* stuff. It was a collection of cock-ups between our players, a case of "*After you, Claude*"'. There is a budding treatise on sociology lurking in Joe Royle's discourse here, but the central image is of an opposition defence so under-employed that they have time for more than a breather. If defenders are having a ridiculously easy time of it the *cigars* in question will invariably be *fat*, and the keeper may even be able to have *a read of the paper*.

Snow: Perhaps used more of Garryowens in rugby, but if a clearance or long through ball has gone very high you might say that it has *snow on it*, even if you are commentating in Guadalajara.

So-called fans: A common way of describing the **hooligan** *element,* adopted by those who wish both to show their contempt for the *tiny minority* and to allege that not being a proper fan ranks very high among their possible sins. See also **lesser nations**.

Soccer: A noun shunned by commentators who fear they might sound American if they use it too often.

Yet, like 'rugger', it's a good old English contraction –
in this case of *Association Football*. Alliteration
helped the noun survive through the 1980s when
there was talk of the '*Soccer Sixes* Tournament' and
soccer stars helped youngsters with *soccer skills*. But
soccer sucked when, later, *football* came home.

Socceroo: The *Socceroo* is a cross between a footballer
and an animal. Kevin Muscat is an example of the
species. The language of football is often playful and
inventive when it comes to describing the meeting
of two cultures. Hybrids like *El Tel* and *McBerti*
have resulted, some with more lasting appeal than
others.

Socks: Since more stringent regulations came into
force, players like Frank Lampard sr, Soren Lerby or
Maxime Bossis cannot advertise themselves by their
permanently *rolled down socks*. But while FIFA have
forced players to pull their *socks* up, managers like
Graeme Souness prefer their teams to work them *off*:
'I am not big on systems or tactics. I am big on great
players working their *socks off*'. It is still possible to
make metaphorical reference to other bits of kit
('Tony Pulis said he knew his team had to *roll their
sleeves up* and *battle*') but the loss of your *socks* is now
the much-preferred indicator of a high *work-rate*:
'The manager brings out stats on the distances the
players travel during a game, and they are running
their *socks off*, *box-to-box*'. Note a variant from Alex
Ferguson: 'The *lads* have run their *socks* into the
ground'.

Soft: Even though there are fewer *hard men* than in
bygone days, footballers still don't care for anything
soft: 'It was a really *soft goal*'; 'Carbone was guilty of
another *soft offside*'. This adjective is useful to commentators who wish to criticise while avoiding

morally portentous words like 'bad' or 'unforgivable'
– which is what *soft* means here.

Soho Square: Located *in the heart of London's
West End* (as they like to inform us, especially before
cup draws), the address is no less innocuous a
synecdoche for FA headquarters than was *Lancaster
Gate*. But there have been times when journalism
has made it seem more than an incidental backdrop,
and the location has become something like an expla-
nation for the goings-on there. It is a sign of the
waning influence of the Football League that nobody
seems to care what people get up to in *Lytham
St Anne's*.

Solitary: Comes across as more emphatic than 'one' or
'single' in the following examples: 'Blackburn *pipped*
United to the title by a *solitary* point'; 'Houston is the
*solitary **survivor*** from the 1976 final'; 'Hakan Sukur is
the *solitary* striker' (although ***lone*** is preferable in this
context).

Something: In football this means *one point*: 'We
deserved to get *something* out of the game, even if we
weren't expecting to *come away* with a victory'.

Space: Like ***width***, a noun much used and appreci-
ated in modern football parlance. *Space* can be measured by the *acre* or the *ocean*: 'Canoville found himself
in *acres* of *space* there'. Good passes not only find
their *intended targets*, but find them *in space*. ***Class***
players always seem to manage to *find* or *create* or
make space for themselves, just as they seem to have
more ***time*** *on the ball* than lesser mortals: 'Rivaldo
made space for himself with a ***sublime*** dummy'.

Spearhead: Denotes the target man who either
*ploughs a lone **furrow*** up front or who provides a

platform for others to play off: 'Shearer will *spearhead* the attack with Bellamy *playing* just *off* him'. Preferred to the verb *head*, which has other uses, and broadly synonymous with *lead*, except that a striker who *spearheads* the attack, rather than just *leading the line*, is made to sound that bit more potent and dangerous.

Special one: At the first press conference he gave as Chelsea manager, Jose Mourinho merely called himself 'a' *special one*. That was not quite *special* enough for the media who have since afforded him the definite article. The phrase, with its slightly translated flavour, pays suitable tribute to the epitome of the sophisticated foreign manager. But that coat is from Matalan.

Specialist: 'Anderton will have to see a *specialist*'. This is an infallible, economic way of indicating that an injury sustained by a footballer promises to **rule** him **out** for a long while. It is not always necessary to specify what kind of *specialist* the ailing player has to see, unless it's *a Harley Street specialist*. Injury permitting, players can be *dead-ball specialists*, and teams *draw specialists*.

Speculative: When executed from some distance, shots, and *lobs* in particular it would seem, may be described as *speculative* – whether they result in a goal or not. When they do, the adjective removes some of the acclaim with which a *long-range* **effort** would normally be greeted by suggesting politely there might have been an element of good fortune: 'Ronaldinho's *speculative* **effort caught** England **cold**'. The noun *speculation* is usually preceded in football talk by *transfer*, a circumstance which will invariably *unsettle* the player in question even if the opportunity is *rebuffed*.

Spice: Any appetising fixture becomes even more so if there is *added spice* caused by *history* between the two clubs. Very often the *spice* is not especially piquant: 'The fact that Lee Clark is a lifelong Newcastle fan simply *adds spice* to this North East *derby*'. Compare *ironically*.

Spill: The most likely word – ahead of *fumble*, which has oval-ball connotations – for a goalkeeper's failing to clasp or hold on to the ball at a critical moment: 'Martyn *spilt* Scholes's deflected free-kick to Ronaldo, who scored at *nudging* range'. Predictably it's no use crying by the time the spillage has occurred.

Spin: *On the spin* is preferred in football to *in a row*, as in this dizzying piece of writing: 'The London-born hitman *bagged* his fifth goal of the season to send Burnley *spiralling* to their fourth defeat *on the spin*'. Synonyms are *on the bounce*, *back-to-back* and *on the trot*. This last phrase featured in the following curious sentence spotted in a broadsheet: 'Unpredictable Manchester City have now lost seven games *on the trot* and have not won in fifteen'.

Spine: The phrase *good spine* signifies a team blessed with a reliable goalkeeper, central defender, *ball-winner* and centre-forward: 'There's a *good spine* to the team with Andy Hessenthaler back in midfield'.

Splinters: What you get if you are *out of favour* and have been *warming the bench* too often instead of getting *first-team football*.

Spoil the party: Very common in end-of-season football reporting, this is the uncharitable act of teams with the audacity not to *read the script*, and to draw against or even beat opponents celebrating a feat like promotion or a championship win: 'Norwich nearly *spoilt the party* with an equalising goal, but Davis **grabbed** a late winner for the *exultant* champions'.

Spoils: Although the winner of a war traditionally takes all the *spoils*, in football parlance the metaphor tends to be used to provide an alternative to *draw*: 'Paul Simpson and David Hodgson were happy with *a share of the spoils* in the **battle** of the *basement boys* at Brunton Park.'

Sporting: Only in the English language does *sporting* denote a moral attitude as well as a physical disposition. It is therefore used sparingly in the British game. Like tweeds, the term is more common among continentals than among the English whose conduct they would emulate. Though the **likes of** Sporting Lisbon borrow an English term, it is a term no English club has in its title.

Spot: When referees pick up a piece of foul play they are praised for a good *spot* or are said to be *spot on*: '*Shirtpulling* was a *good spot* by Mr Frisk there'. Occasionally the phrase is also used to denote the **vision** necessary for a good pass. The Big-Ronism was *spotter's badge*.

Spot kick: Alternative to **penalty** which tends to be used only in the singular, mainly in the course of ninety minutes. This is curious given that the *dreaded* penalty shoot-outs are not really penalising anything (other than the failure of teams to beat one another) and *spot kick* might in this case be more apposite.

Sprawling: Describes a fairly desperate *save* or *stop*: 'The Gillingham keeper made a brilliant 57th-minute *sprawling stop* to fingertip a Tonge free kick *special* round the post.' Used when the commentator

or journalist did not think the keeper was going to
make it.

Spray: Steven Gerrard qualifies as a person who can
spray 30-yard passes *at will*. *Ping* is an alternative.
Sometimes the activity can become fairly ineffectual
though: 'They're really *spraying it around* and if anything nobody is *putting their foot* on it'.

Spring: The generic noun for a player's ability to *get
up* in the air: 'Scholes has such *great spring* for a little
man'. With the verb, you can *spring* a *surprise* or
the *offside trap* (or both at the same time if you were
playing against George Graham's Arsenal).

Squad number: The final ignominy for an *out-of-
favour* player is not to be *assigned a squad number*.
This way you really can become ***anonymous***.

Square: To cross the ball – 'Galvin *squared* to
Stapleton' – but also to equalise: 'Romario *squared*
two minutes later'. Defences which tend to **step up**
can be *caught square* by a **killer ball**.

Square one: While the language of football borrows
extensively from other idioms for its own metaphorical purposes, *back to square one* is for once a phrase
that has travelled in the other direction. The expression was endowed to the English language by football
commentators in the early days of radio when a pitch
was divided up into different squares in a plan
printed in the *Radio Times* to ease the strain on the
imagination of the listeners. *Back to square one* sig-
nalled that the ball was with the goalkeeper and
another **passage** *of play* was about to start. But it
seems now to have left the language of football for
good. Exasperated managers prefer instead to go back
to the *drawing board* or the **training ground**.

Squeaky-bum time: 'It's getting tickly now –
squeaky-bum time, I call it'. This celebrated phrase was
coined in 2003 during a title *run-in*, although it may
be considered more appropriate for nerve-wracking
developments at the bottom end of the table. Initially,
the expression was so associated with Alex Ferguson
that any allusion to it was preceded with a comment
like 'as the manager of Manchester United once
so wisely put it'. Now it is a well-established way
of announcing a crunch moment in football –
'Angola's *squeaky-bum **encounter*** with Rwanda is on
8 November' – and in other arenas: 'Splendid bowling
by McGrath and, given that Ian Bell is next, this is
officially *squeaky-bum time* for England'.

Squirm: Unfortunate goalkeepers allow the ball to
squirm, often ***agonisingly***, under their bodies or
through their hands. *Squirt* and *squeeze* complete the
series.

Stab: How to finish from close range: 'After
good work by Pennant, Smith *stabbed* the ball home'.
The usage could also hide the suggestion of a ***toe-
poke***. Synonyms include *jab home*, *poke home* and
prod home.

Stadium: When clubs move to a new *ground* (Bolton,
Reading, Sunderland are just a few examples) they
tend these days to call it a *stadium*, as though this
auspicious name were more likely to attract *big nights*
of cosmopolitan action. Here the language of football
has bifurcated, for fans persist in talking about *football grounds*, while people in suits, like architects and
directors, call them *stadia*.

Stalemate: Synonymous with *deadlock*, but, while
the latter is *there to be broken*, a *stalemate* is more
obdurate or enduring. Indeed, the noun can mean

both a result (a draw, obviously) as well as the conditions leading to that result. 'Jenkins has broken the *deadlock* at Vicarage Road, but it's drifting towards a *stalemate* at Prenton Park'. Whereas in chess *stalemate* marks the end of the game and the clocks are turned off, the term can be used at any point during the ninety minutes of football.

Stall: Always *set out* by a team **early** *doors* when *signalling their intent*, usually with hardworking defensive play. The term is used so routinely and with such faint praise that there is no real indication of what is on the *stall*: 'They've come here and they've *set their stall out* and you have to take your hat off to them'.

Stanchion: Corner-frame of the goalpost only ever mentioned when the ball gets stuck in it, which happens on average every twenty years, so that our spelling of this word is provisional. Trevor Brooking, and the keeper who had to dislodge the ball back then, probably know the Hungarian word for it though.

Stand: The verb is a common shorthand in commentary when you wonder whether a goal will be allowed: 'Saha's looking round at the linesman but it will *stand*'; 'They're busy celebrating but it won't *stand*'. The noun of course refers to the *stand* of a football ground, curious in that it used to be the only place to sit. Now that grounds are enclosed on all sides, *stands* are mentioned specifically only when managers are sent off and watch in **exile** *from the stands*, or when a commentator softens criticism by reminding us that the game is *easy from the stands* or *easy from up here*. *Grandstand finishes* can happen in football, but the expression always seems home-sick for athletics or horse-racing from where it is imported.

Star name: The phrase usually appears in the plural
when the players to whom it refers are unlikely to
appear – 'Manchester United will be without several
of their *star names* for the *visit* of Birmingham' – and
when attendance at a testimonial is being drummed
up: 'Several *star names* had been promised at Sean
O'Driscoll's testimonial'.

Starlet: Typically a young, up-and-coming player
who is good, but not good enough yet to be called
a star. Also sometimes the star player at an *unfashionable* club: 'McSporran, the Wycombe *starlet*…'.
Besides, 'the Wycombe Star' sounds uncomfortably
like a local paper.

Static: What defences can be when not reacting to
the *movement* of the attacking team, while goalkeepers similarly guilty of not moving with sufficient
speed tend to be described as *flat-footed*. *Statuesque*
is an acceptable synonym: 'The *former* Hucknall
Town striker *drifted* past the *statuesque* Jinadu with
embarrassing ease'.

Stature: In football parlance the metaphor *grow in
stature* is often used of defenders, especially if they
are young. The timeframe can be a *game* or a *season*.
'After a shaky start against the *physical* **presence**
of Emile Heskey, the Villa centre-backs Olof Mellberg
and Liam Ridgewell *grew in stature*'.

Step up: Denotes the activity of a defence which
moves forward in unison to catch an opposing striker
offside: 'The Pompey **back four** stepped up quickly
there again'. *Squeeze up* is a variant. Also used (often
as a noun) to describe the **gulf in class** between one
division and another or to indicate the vertigo likely
to be experienced by a player *adjusting* to a higher
division: 'It's a *massive step-up* for Zamora from the

Withdean Stadium'. *Step up*, with 'to the plate' under-stood as in baseball, is applied to anybody who *takes responsibility*; the locution is particularly apt during the *dreaded* penalty shoot-out.

Stick: Strikers are often reported to have *stuck it* (whether the chance or the ball) *away* with **aplomb**. The noun refers to the 'post', more often the *back stick* than the other one: 'At Dundee United I'd been very much a *back-stick* player, but Saunders got me to be less **static**, to attack the *near post* as often as I could'. Players can also *get a lot of stick* in the dressing room, although this is used in a playful sense these days for something like a **dodgy** haircut. Real criticism would earn you an *earful* or *harsh* **words**.

Stiffs: Slang-term with a wide scope of reference, including dead people, slow horses, manual labourers and reserve football teams. Even if still not permitted in official journalese, fans and fanzines use the term so routinely that they ignore its wider connotations: 'Murray has been *turning it on* for the *stiffs* of late and deserves his chance'; 'We had to let him go as there was no point him *burning up* in the *stiffs*'.

Sting: Good, but perhaps rather complacent, teams are *stung into action* by an unexpected goal against them. *Piledrivers*, or *howitzers*, *sting* the hands of the keeper. Though impressive, this is substantially less than what the real things would do to his hands.

Stinker: These days used of referees more often than players, who will have had a *nightmare* if given a **torrid time**.

Stone-cold: Or should it be *stonewall*? The following report hardly resolves the issue: ' "From where I stood

it looked a *stonewall* penalty", said Danny Wilson of
MK Dons. Surprisingly, Walsall boss Paul Merson
agreed, saying "it was a *stone-cold* penalty" '. And if
Wilson had proposed *stick-on*, we like to think Merson
would have come back with *nailed on*. Wilson says
cast-iron, and Merson says *sure-fire*. But, for once, an
undisputed *penalty*.

Stood up tall: For goalkeepers a synonym for *made
himself big*. These idioms work as such only in the
past tense.

Stoppage: Used most commonly in the plural or else
in the familiar phrase *stoppage time*: 'Roger Milford
has added three minutes for *stoppages*'. The *stoppages*
in question were not called this while they were hap-
pening. Commentators meanwhile wait for a *break in
play* or a moment when play is *held up* to read out the
line-ups or turn to their summariser.

Stop-start: Describes *drab affairs* where there is no
rhythm or pattern to the game: 'It was a real *stop-start
affair* until the first goal came'. Can also be employed
to describe the travails of a player who is injured or
out of *favour*: 'I had a real *stop-start* first season at
the club'. As *kick-start* is preferred to 'relaunch', so
stop-start is preferred to 'interrupted'.

Storm: The figurative *storms* a team *weathers* (*storms*
are never mentioned unless they are *weathered*)
tend to be *early*, whereas *scares* can occur either
early or late in a game. Conversely, the adjective
storming tends to be reserved for *second half come-
backs* or *passages* of play where teams *up the
tempo*.

Straight: A *straight red* is distinct from a red which
is the product of two *yellows*. When a player comes on

as a substitute for someone in the same position, it is unfailingly hailed as a *straight swap*. But, unlike the Panini stickers which feature them, footballers tend to be *exchanged* rather than *swapped* in the transfer market: 'Blinker goes to Celtic in a cash-plus-player *exchange* deal'.

Stranded: The unfortunate fate of keepers who race from their line or come for crosses, only to see the ball go past them into the *unguarded net*: 'Seven minutes later Malbranque *turned **provider*** with a penetrating forward pass that Saha slipped past the *stranded* Seaman'. Compare **no man's land**.

Strength: Common in two phrases. Teams are invariably *at full strength* if they have no injuries. *Strength in depth* is the magical property deemed necessary to succeed in the age of squad **rotation** and fixture *pile-ups*. It is the stumbling block for clubs who merely have a good team but are not so unfair as to keep in their own reserves personnel who could *walk into* another club's starting **eleven**.

Strides: The unit of measure for an improving side: 'As Wales prepare for the **lottery** of the play-offs, coach Mark Hughes reflected yesterday on the *strides* his team have made over the last two years'. These *strides* are often *great* or *massive*. And when a manager talks about 'how far we have *travelled* in so short a space of time', he is not referring to the speed of the **team bus** but alluding to the progress his side have made on the pitch.

Strike: Perhaps the most common word for a shot which results in a goal: 'What a *strike*!' Sometimes it almost seems to describe the psychological effect on the opposition as well as the obvious effect on the scoreline: 'As Stockport strove to force the win,

Gardner *struck* against the **run of play** with ten
minutes left'. There are other terms which more
colourfully draw out the analogy between a powerful
shot and an artillery piece: 'Wark *let fly* with a
cannonball shot'; 'A Dean Whitehead *thunderbolt*
flew into the top corner'; 'Robben scored another
cracker from the 18-yard line'; 'It was a veritable
howitzer from the stocky Bulgarian'. Compare
screamer. The *fireworks* can always go off, either
when there is a burst of goals or a *22-man* **brawl**, but
blasts and **rockets** tend to be more associated with
managers than hotshots.

String: When a goalkeeper is *kept busy*, he may need
to *pull off* a *string* of good or even *stunning* saves.
Influential players, especially **midfield generals** if
they don't mind mixing metaphors, *pull the strings*.

Strip: What footballers wear, or used to. *Strips* are
being supplanted by *kits*. Until recently, at least according to the specifications noted in football annuals,
a *strip* included *jerseys* and *stockings*, rather than
shirts and **socks**. Substitutes are told to *strip off* by
the manager. They don't need to be told that this
means only the tracksuit.

Stroke of half-time: Goals which go in after about
45 minutes are, emphatically and precisely, scored
on the stroke of half-time, even if half-time can be
announced only by the referee's whistle.

Strong: Managers trying *kidology* will often demand
a *strong referee* for a game *in the lion's den* (which
sometimes will actually be Millwall's). *Strong hand*
is a specific expression used when the keeper makes
a save from a fierce shot if he would normally
be expected only to **get a hand to it** as it passed by
him.

Studs: In *almighty* scrambles, the *studs* tend to *fly* – indeed the image can be used in a wider sense to describe a game where the tackles become *x-rated*: 'After the *nonsense* involving Sammy Nelson, the *studs* began to *fly* all over the *park*'. If Sir Alex Ferguson's *hairdryer treatment* does not work, *studs* can even *fly* in the dressing room. *Studs up*, or *studs high*, can describe any robust challenge, but particularly one where a player has *gone over the top*: 'The next significant act was a brutish, *studs-high* tackle by Alan Smith'. In a similar usage, a player can be said to *show his studs* (in the direction of a player's backside rather than to the fourth *official*).

Stuff: A word that appears many times in this lexicon. Its most basic meaning tends to be *football* as in *great stuff, lovely stuff*. The past participle of the verb, on the other hand, is used when you have not played so well and been soundly beaten. Curiously, managers whose teams have been *stuffed* can confess to being *gutted*.

Style: Invariably *turned on*, whenever a team is playing *exhibition stuff*. Managers like to think they can instil a certain *style of play* in their charges. Commentators meanwhile like to observe a *contrast in styles* if a British team is playing a *technically* accomplished foreign side. Compare *way*.

Sublime: Reserved for those consummate moments of individual skill, which might be a *dinked finish* or a *cushioned volley*. *Exquisite*, perhaps for a *first touch* or a *floated pass* is hardly less refined. *Sumptuous* is another adjective becoming as fashionable as the menus of certain ex-footballers turned restaurateurs.

Substitution: Should a substitute score or perhaps play a conspicuous part in a goal, the *substitution* turns out to be *inspired*. *Last throw of the dice* is the standard rhetorical description of a manager's final *substitution*, even if he can make further tactical *changes*. See also *super-sub*.

Suck in: A classic cliché employed more sparingly nowadays: 'For all the attempts of the Feethams *faithful* to *suck the ball in*, it was a poor display'. But you can still talk about teams being *sucked into* the relegation zone.

Super-sub: A phrase which first seemed to come into vogue for the comet that was David Fairclough; now said routinely of any player who *climbs off the bench* to score, often without the implication, once promoted by Fairclough and other *super-subs* of the 1970s, that they were much less effective if included in the *starting eleven*. However the moniker can still be unwanted for this reason: 'Paul Peschisolido fears he will be *saddled* with the *tag* of *super-sub* again after *climbing off the bench* to complete Derby's comeback against Coventry'.

Surprise package: Always a nice surprise – every year there seems to be at least one team in each division who are seen to be exceeding expectations over a season: 'In the first half Nigel Worthington's *men* were outplayed by the First Division's *surprise package* Wigan'.

Survival: *Survival* would seem to be a modest ambition, a basic *sine qua non*, but, in football parlance, the term again carries its own implicit cargo: *survival* here means 'not being relegated'. *Staying alive* in the cup may be merely a distraction in these circumstances: 'It's nice to be in the hat for the fifth round, but we all know *survival* is the priority here'. Which translates as: 'I can't believe we're still in this cup, because I get sacked if we go down'. *Safety* is a slightly less emotive term. Italians talk of *la salvezza* or 'salvation' in this context.

Survivor: Overblown expression, particularly in the light of real disasters such as the Munich air crash, to indicate a player who is still at a club where *honours* were won at an earlier time: 'Tony Adams is the only *survivor* of that double-winning side'. After the death of Diana, Princess of Wales, an edict went to the commentators of the first match to be played (Bradford City v Sunderland) informing them to be careful not to say 'the shot went straight into the wall' or to talk of Phillips' 'killer instinct'. *Sudden death*, however, remains the potentially insensitive description of what happens if the first five penalties of a shoot-out have been taken inconclusively.

Sweet: An adjective primarily used with *volley* to indicate a particularly aesthetic *contact*, but can be used of any shot or pass. An especially *sweet volley* becomes *sublime*.

Switch: When wingers change sides (*flanks* that is, not teams), they *switch* from right to left or *vice versa*. An ability to *switch the play* and *spray* a pass *into space*, often with *vision*, is the hallmark of a *creative* footballer. *Half-time* is sometimes referred to as the *switch* (when teams change ends): 'Mali will want to make a *change*, I'll wager, but not till after the *switch*'.

Swoop: Adopted when a team moves to complete a quick transfer (or even when they don't). The verb may be combined with the nickname of the club doing the *swooping* to create a comically literal effect: 'The Robins have *swooped in* on Shelton' or 'Grasshoppers *swoop* for Littbarski'. Like the term *capture*,

also widely used for transfer *acquisitions*, this terminology perhaps originated in a period before football
agents became all-powerful.

System: Most common way of referring to the formation a team uses. For example, it may *abandon* a *sweeper
system* to go to an **orthodox** back four. In recent years,
we also find mention of *squad systems* or **rotation**
systems which managers operate when their teams are
still in several competitions. Scouts always seem to
be employed as part of a *scouting system* (which may
simply mean Dave Sexton working part-time).

T

Tackle: Good strong *tackles* should be described as
crunching, shuddering, robust, rumbustious or (particularly if a continental referee should award a free
kick as a result) *British* – in all the above cases
you may roll the 'r' in an attempt at onomatopoeia.
With weak *tackles*, some of the available adjectives
or adjectival phrases are: *flimsy, spineless, pathetic
excuse for a*. If the *tackle* is illegal but thought to
have been a **genuine** *attempt* to play the ball, it is
described as *not malicious* or **mistimed** (as opposed to
late, which indicates a degree of malice afore-
thought). If the *tackle* is really bad, it can produce
euphemisms such as *poor, over-robust, scything, not
the best of*, or provoke condemnation as *appalling,
shocking, disgraceful*. The *sliding tackle* is notable as
being a technical rather than an evaluative expression. Note that the act of *tackling back* does not
necessarily involve actual *tackling*, but rather getting
behind the ball when the other side has it. See also
challenge.

Take each game as it comes: One of the select group of clichés, almost on a par with *sick as a parrot*, that is seldom resorted to by anybody in the game without the qualification that it is the *old cliché*. A similar idea is: 'I can promise you we are not *looking past* our next league game on Saturday against Stockport'.

Take the result: The obligatory post-match interview throws up some formulae of its own. When managers or players profess to be satisfied with a result which, like a slim first-leg lead or a draw, is not obviously satisfying, the standard method for so doing consists of hypothetically *taking* that same result, had it been *offered* before the match: 'The **lads** are not exactly dancing on the ceiling, but if you'd *offered* us the point before today's game, we'd have *taken* it'. A harmless surmise, but not to be made by anyone with a match-fixing case pending.

Take up: Much preferred to 'adopt' or 'assume' in football when praising a player for finding **space** and being available for a pass: 'Van Nistelrooy always *takes up* such *good positions* **off the back** of the defenders'.

Talismanic: More common in adjectival form than as a noun. Pertains usually to a striker with a habit of scoring important goals, and also to any player who can *turn a match*. These key men can also be described as the *heartbeat* or the *standard-bearer* of the team.

Talking point: Tends to be *major*, and in the era of punditry is filed away for discussion *after the game*. But at half- or full-time a commentator will often proudly hand over to the studio panel with words such as 'plenty of *talking points* there', as though he has been responsible for making their job easier.

Tap-in: 'Craney completed the rout with a *tap-in*'. Borrowed from golf, this is probably the most common of a range of terms to register an easy finish, even though it is often further qualified as *simple* or *the simplest of*. The equivalent for a headed goal is a *nod-in*: 'Drogba leapt high above a **static** defence to *nod-in* from Duff's corner'.

Tap up: 'The latest *tapping-up* affair puts Peter Kenyon in a very poor light'; 'Alex Inglethorpe resigned amid allegations he was using his England job to *tap up* other clubs' players'. The official term for trying to *unsettle* players under contract by dangling the carrot of a move is an *illegal approach*, but *tapping up* is the ubiquitous colloquialism.

Target: Strikers both are the *target* – 'we need a *target-man* in the team, *in the **mould** of* Mark Falco' – and are expected to hit it. But *target* is used most commonly in football parlance to mean the goal, when it is missed: 'From that position, you've really got to *hit the target* – Tarantini should have *made* the keeper *work* there'.

Teacups: 'Once West Ham went ahead the only remaining doubt concerned the number of *teacups* Pardew had needed to hurl across the dressing room at half-time to get them going.' The interval cuppa is often a prop for a motivational fracas.

Team affairs: Phrase only to be used during interregna when the **caretaker**-*manager* presides. Almost archetypally: 'David Pleat takes charge of *team affairs* until a new manager can be found'. Interesting in that the new manager would not normally be expected to run the **PLC** as well as *team affairs*.

Team bus: Stirling *Albion* took their name from a company which built buses and trucks, some of which were once parked behind the goal at Annfield to form a makeshift stand. From the day Mourinho could not hide his exasperation at Santini's ultra-defensive tactics, the *team bus* could be *parked* in front of the goal too, metaphorically speaking. Although the *bus* in question stood in the way that day, Tottenham's coach left soon after.

Technical: Particularly prevalent in the upper eche-lons of European and international football. Teams whose individual players are blessed with all the req-uisite skills (they have *great technique*) are *technically* accomplished. Sometimes praise in these terms barely camouflages the suspicion that a team may not be the sum of its parts. Or the *technical* merits of a team may implicitly draw you to its temperamental deficiencies: 'The Croats are *technically* very gifted, but they don't seem to have the stomach for a fight'. Nevertheless, the recently invented dotted lines that restrict the touchline movement of agitated managers have been dignified by the term *technical area*, evidence that the adjective continues to live and thrive beyond suspi-cion. Note also another adverbial usage meaning 'theoretically': '*Technically*, that has to *go down* as a chance', the implication being that nobody could have been expected to score.

Telegraph: When a player *telegraphs* the pass – that is, he betrays his intentions far too obviously to the opposition – the telegraphy in question is presumably the semaphore signalling of old, rather than the more recent and familiar tapping of keys which does not involve overt signalling of intention.

Tempers: Invariably *fray*.

Tempo: The pace at which the team as a *collective unit* is said to play. Usually English teams are exhorted to *up the tempo* and to play with *more* or *higher tempo*. More occasionally you can pause to admire the *lovely tempo* or *samba rhythm* of more patient **build-up** *play*.

Tempting: Describes crosses, with the understanding that it is the striker who is *tempted* to *apply a finishing touch*, though there may be circumstances in which a keeper is *tempted* to leave his line for a cross he cannot reach. It is more usual on these occasions to describe the cross as *teasing*.

Terraces: Once, when stadiums consisted largely of *terraces*, an innocuous synonym for a football ground but, now that all-seaters are the norm, usually invoked as implicit proof of the loyalty and longevity of a football fan: 'I stood on the *terraces* of the Gallowgate back then'. Fathers (and any shoulders onto which a child may have been lifted or rolled-up newspapers which may have been urinated through) should be mentioned in these cases too. Politicians are particularly fond of mentioning the *terraces* they helped to destroy.

Terrier: Describes energetic midfield players. Perhaps it is our imagination but the phrase often seems to be used of redheads like Alan Ball, Billy Bremner and Paul Scholes.

Territory: Employed much less than in rugby, although occasionally you hear of teams being unable to *translate* their *territorial advantage* into goals. But one usage that is very common occurs if a free kick is conceded 20 to 25 yards from goal: 'This is Neil Clement *territory*, Ron'. *Country* is available too, possibly with a twist of irony in international matches.

Terrorise: Unchecked by the events of 9/11, centre-forwards (usually *bustling* ones, good in the air) continue to *terrorise* defenders, while wingers tend merely to *embarrass* their **opposite numbers**.

Test: Verb which in recent usage means to submit to a *fitness test* – 'Coventry *test* Jenkinson and Lightbourne..' – but otherwise traditionally applied to goalkeepers: 'Cascarino *tested* the keeper from 25 yards'. It's always a *test* the keeper seems to pass.

Textbook: *Textbook* appears as an adjective in certain football contexts, most commonly when a *textbook finish* results in a goal. It is difficult to imagine a football *textbook* or lexicon finding many readers.

Thank: When a keeper has played better than his team and *got them out of jail*, he can be commended in the following terms: 'Spurs have Thorstvedt *to thank* for a *share of the spoils*'.

The: A few exalted clubs enjoy the privilege of a definite article before their names – *The Arsenal, The Villa, The Albion* (*Th'Albion* in local vernacular), *The Wednesday* (their proud name till 1929). Teams known habitually by a plural may also be called *The Spurs* or *The Wolves*, but, in general, the article should be omitted. When someone says something like 'I love Stoke', confusion can occur (as well as surprise), for do they mean City or city? Italian averts potential confusion by insisting on the definite article when you're talking about a team which is or could be a place (hence *La Roma, Il Lecce*), but English allays it by making the subject plural, hence 'Liverpool *are* rich', 'Newcastle *were* lucky'. There is no surer way of betraying ignorance of football than that of using a singular instead. But there is an exception: when, after the success of the Euro '96 song *Football's*

Coming Home, fans adopted this tune for their own purposes, the metre forced the plural to become singular. Hence: 'We're going up, we're going up, *City's* going up'.

Theatrical: Awed commentators, delighted to have been chosen for a *big European night* ahead of their colleague left behind at Oakwell, refer to grand, historic football grounds as *theatres*. But the adjective *theatrical* in the mouths of the same commentators is unfailingly, puritanically pejorative. *Theatrical* equals inauthentic, unconvincing, histrionic: 'Maric took a *theatrical* tumble, but the ref **waved** it **away**'. References to *Hollywood* often follow, an obvious **dive** earning a remark like: 'that won't be *winning any Oscars*' or 'that was *pure Hollywood*'. There seem to be other academies with advanced forms of *simulation* on the syllabus: 'Hunt has obviously studied at the Reebok Stadium *School for the Dramatic Arts* because he *tumbled* to the floor like a man trying to walk a tightrope in clogs'. But the words *drama* and *dramatic*, used especially of *starts* and *finishes*, tend not to be used self-consciously: 'What *drama* here in the final minutes as Barnsley score again'.

Things: In football, means **silverware** – 'I've come to this **football club** to win *things*' – or bad press - 'There's been a few *things* said in the media but that's just spurred us on, to be honest' – or *pieces of business*: 'Other players can only dream of the *things* he does in training'.

Thoughts: International managers are perceived to be more thoughtful than others, as they consider players who are on the verge of **recognition**: 'Scott Parker is certain to be in Sven's *thoughts*'. **Domestic** managers are more likely to have prosaic-sounding

plans, usually mentioned with negative conse-
quences: 'I'm sorry for the *lad*. But Andy Todd is not
part of our *plans*'.

Thrash: Good *thrashings*, *thumpings* or *hidings* can
all still be administered on the football pitch, despite
the fact that corporal punishment is no longer permitted, even in public schools. Note a celebrated
Nordic variant: 'Your *boys* took *one helluva beating*'.
Once players *slap in* a transfer request, a deal on a
new contract is then *thrashed out*.

Thread: A player who can produce a *defence-splitting*
through ball needs no training in needlework:
'Downing *threaded* a *perfectly weighted* pass into the
path of Queudrue, who finished with some *aplomb*'.
Some reporters, though, should really sign on for an
extra lesson in overstitch: 'Nolan *threaded* the neatest
of passes through the *eye* of Fulham's defensive *needle*'. *Needle* is more apposite when it refers to a sense
of niggling aggression creeping into a game, even if
this is not exactly in the *right spirit*.

Thriller: Any game with a 4–3 scoreline is almost
inevitably described as a 'seven-goal *thriller*' in
despatches, even when the losing side has scored an
academic consolation *deep* in *injury time*. *Thrills*
always seem to be synonymous with goals in football
so that a very exciting one-all draw would rather be
described as *absorbing*. And while *thrillers* tend to be
very close *affairs* decided by the *odd goal* in seven or
nine, more partisan reporting can use the term for
games which eventually become one-sided, as in this
summary of a 3–8 scoreline in the Carling Cup: 'Even
the most fanciful script-writer would have struggled
to come up with anything quite like the 11-goal
thriller which kept us right on the edge of our seats
from start to finish'. Most of the home fans had left

the edge of their seats long before the tenth and eleventh goals went in.

Throw: 'Incredibly, City were gifted their opener when Sorensen as good as *threw* the ball into the net, in a virtual *carbon copy* of the goal at Villa Park'. While actual examples of a keeper accidentally *throwing* the ball into his goal string out laugh-a-minute videos narrated by Rory McGrath, the expression normally just indicates a *howler*: 'Paul Kee was *throwing them in* at about one every match before he fortunately broke his finger'.

Throw men forward: Urgent, desperate teams *throwing caution to the wind*, towards the end of matches which are slipping out of their grasp, do so by *throwing men forward*. The projected men in question are usually more reticent midfielders and sedentary defenders, though goalkeepers are known to *come up* for a final set piece. The idiom modulates slightly should the opposition *go down the other end and score* in these circumstances. Then the unfortunate team is said to be guilty of having *committed too many players forward*.

Tidy: While defenders *tidy up* at the back and forwards *finish tidily*, it is midfielders who are most likely to get credit for actually being *tidy*: 'A hardworking, *tidy* midfielder, Dalla Bona was a prolific scorer for Chelsea's youth and reserve teams'. A hint of faint praise may sometimes surface, but being *tidy* is much better than being plain *honest*.

Time: Since *extra-time* is specifically the half hour appended to unresolved cup ties, the time added on to the ninety minutes is ingeniously known as *time added on*. It is not usual to talk about 'additional time', but it is possible to say 'there will be three *additional minutes*', particularly since the introduction of the *fourth official*'s board. *Time added on* may also be known as *injury time* or *stoppage time* as opposed to *proper time*. Good players will *time* a run *to perfection* (never 'perfectly'), while the adverb *timely* is always combined with *interception*, or more occasionally **intervention**. Finally, it is a miracle how some footballers always seem to have *time on the ball*.

Today's evidence: 'On *today's evidence* they will be really struggling come the end of the season'; 'On *today's evidence* they really need added *firepower* up front'. Means 'after this game' but helps to lend to punditry a forensic dimension.

Toe-poke: From the playground to the training ground, a term of abuse in that all the coaching manuals instruct players to shoot with the *laces*. Reference to a *toe-poke* at professional level is therefore often an indicator of a rushed or faulty finish, in the same category as those goals where the ball is *shinned* in. However, the consummate striker never forgets the most elementary tricks of the trade: 'Crespo produced a super chipped *toe-poke* of a first-time finish'; 'Andrew Cole jinked between Tony Popovic and Michael Hughes before lifting what he modestly labelled a "little *toe-ender*" into the net'.

Tone: The *tone* of a game is often *set* by a *crunching* *tackle* or some *afters*.

Too good to go down: Commentators sensibly eschew the words 'good' and 'bad' in general. But a few clubs in the past were considered *too good to go down*. When they did duly go down, the lucky ones to become *yo-yos*, they left this phrase soaked in hubris. You cannot now venture it without an ironic smile.

No-one seems ever to have said that a team was 'too bad to go up'. Maybe this phrase lacks the assonance and alliteration of the other, or perhaps it would just be bad manners to say so.

Too much: 'Liverpool should *have too much* for Watford'. It is not necessary to specify exactly what Liverpool have *too much* of (indeed it is conventional not to do so), as though it goes without saying. The usage helps then to establish the aura of superiority in question.

Too similar: 'The problem was that Owen and Vassell were clearly *too similar*'. In other words, they make the same kind of runs and tend to get in each other's way or *space*. You would not say that defenders are 'too similar', even when two *hulking* centre-backs without a *yard* of pace between them have been *caught* *square* five times before half-time.

Top: 'When we were walking out for the second half Gordon Hill said to me "I love these *tops*"'. Gordon Hill is not in this example talking about Millwall's new shirts or commenting on the half-time entertainment but referring to the *slickness* of the *playing surface*. If it is wet or greasy *on top*, certain players prefer the extra zip off the pitch and pace on the ball.

Top-flight: 'This is Pearce's fifteenth season in *top-flight* football'. Usefully bridges the self-invented transition between the **Premiership** and the old First Division, or *spells* a player has had in the highest divisions abroad.

Torrid time: Experienced particularly by weak full backs faced by the *mazy runs* or *searing pace* of a winger: 'Giggs was giving young Parnaby a *torrid time* down the left flank'.

Total football: There may be some arguments about the derivation of the phrase (although it will always be associated with the great Dutch sides of the 1970s), but in live commentary it has now become devalued and is used rather lazily whenever a centre-half makes an unexpected *foray*, or someone *pops up* in an unfamiliar position: 'Just look where Lundekvam has ended up in that move. *Total football* from the Saints'. Indeed, some old-school managers positively discourage creative freedom, especially in the defensive third of the field, so that the expression becomes pejorative: 'Yet again we've given the ball away on the edge of our penalty area trying to play "*Total Football*" '.

Track: Can describe the process of marking, especially for forward or midfield players: 'Juninho failed to *track back* and Armstrong took full advantage'. In another usage, managers *track* players, usually for *some time*, with a view to making an offer if they become available.

Tracksuit manager: Denotes not only the choice of clothing favoured by such managers, but also an attitude to the game. You can expect a *tracksuit manager* to have a *hands-on* approach, to love working (*day in day out*) with the players on the **training ground** ('you should see him in the five-a-sides'), and to be having a dispute with his chairman.

Trade: Adopted in connection with the idea of professionalism being a virtue: players *learn* their *trade*, then *know* their *trade*, and only in their autumn years *ply* their *trade*.

Trademark: Used adjectivally in preference to 'characteristic' or 'typical': 'Guppy swung in a *trademark* cross'. Employed also, probably in descending order of frequency, of free kicks, runs, dribbles and shimmies.

Tradition: 'This is a club with a great *tradition*'. Likely to be said fondly by the new manager of a club not faring particularly well in the present, such as Blackpool or Wanderers (if they still exist). Some clubs have a good *cup tradition*. Indeed, the FA Cup in particular attracts all things *traditional*, above all the *traditional* cup-final anthem *Abide With Me*, the *traditional* singing of which is by *tradition* useless. The adjective surfaces sometimes when team **colours** are described – 'West Ham are playing in their *traditional* claret and blue' – and is particularly common if stripes feature – 'Huddersfield, in their *traditional* blue and white stripes'. There seems to be something inherently *traditional* or *familiar* about stripes to the English footballing psyche, perhaps because nearly all the teams that play in stripes were more successful and prominent in the distant past.

Trail: A team first *falls behind* and then tends to *trail* once it is two goals down. The term *trailing leg* is used by partisan commentators to suggest that **contact** was made accidentally rather than because the player *left his foot in*.

Training ground: 'That's one from the *training ground*' is a standard phrase that greets a *well-worked* or perhaps slightly ingenious free kick. For extra emphasis, the phrase *straight off* or *from* is used, to confirm just how well the move has translated itself to a real game: 'Tony Carrs scored the goal of his life *straight off* the *training ground* and left beaten keeper Kevin Dearden stunned'. Players will sometimes corroborate praise for a team-mate by remarking tantalisingly: 'you should see the things he does *in training*'. This is particularly true of out-of-form foreign strikers who knock chances in *for fun* on the *training ground*.

Transfer list: Players are *placed* on this *list* or may be described as *transfer-listed*, even though the list in question seems to be imaginary and certainly not available on the internet.

Transfer window: Once transfer activity was cut off by a *deadline*, and on *deadline day* fans would rush home to teletext to find out which players their club had *shipped* in and out and where John Burridge was going next. Now *wheeling and dealing* must be confined to a *transfer window*. Reporters have therefore begun to work on the idiomatic potential of the new terminology. One contribution comes from a Ceefax scribe who may be recalling a personal encounter with a sash frame: 'Sunderland hope to make another signing before the *transfer window* slams shut'. Another, from Tom Dart of *The Times*, draws, or else we hesitate to think, on a more literary kind of experience: 'The January window passed at Fratton Park without Yakubu Ayegbeni *defenestrating* himself'.

Travelling army: Any *set* of away fans tends to be called a *travelling army*. But although football fans can be violent and destructive, here the image conveys no menace. Indeed, the *Tartan Army*, Scotland's merry band of fans, is always praised for its pacifism and good cheer when it's not smashing up the goalposts at **Wembley**.

Treatment: One of those words that can have opposite meanings depending on the context. Injured players receive *treatment* from the physio, so that the *treatment-table* or *treatment-room* become symbolic: 'The Goodison *treatment-room* is full at the moment, with Ferguson and Gravesen **doubtful**'. But sometimes the reason players take knocks is the *treatment* meted out to them by opponents: 'Young Ronaldo has been on the receiving end of some heavy *treatment* from Kishishev all afternoon'.

Trenches: Imagined in conditional phrases as the location *par excellence* for commitment and stamina, *the trenches* relativise the talents of certain players not known for *digging deep*: 'You wouldn't want Di Canio *in the trenches* with you'. But note going **over the top** means something else in football.

Trickle: A verb to describe the progress of shots where the striker did not **get hold** of it; these usually *trickle harmlessly* to the keeper, but sometimes **agonisingly** *wide* or *over the line*.

Tricky: The favoured adjective for *dribbling **wingers*** or for those away ties, usually against lower opposition, which are a *potential **banana skin***. An away **date** with one of the **big boys** would be called *daunting* or *difficult* rather than *tricky*.

Troop: The verb to describe the ambulation back to the dressing room of a player who has **seen red** or a team losing at half-time: 'The Mariners *trooped* back to their dressing room no doubt expecting a **rocket** from Alan Buckley'.

Trouble: When you have given a penalty away, an alternative to having your *misery **compounded*** by a *yellow card* is to be booked *for your trouble*: 'Evans was *booked for his trouble* and Bruce Dyer added insult to injury by firing the penalty low past keeper Paston's right hand'. In a classic cliché, an inaccurate pass *plays* your team-mate *into trouble*. *Trouble* is also used with various parts of the ***anatomy*** to indicate an injury that *forces a player off* or *continues to keep him out*. It is never quite clear when *groin trouble* becomes a *groin ***problem***.

Trump card: Considering how much time footballers spend in card schools, this metaphor for the best player in a manager's hand is not perhaps as prevalent as you might expect. The use of *ace*, whether up sleeves or not, as a synonym for *striker* is also fairly rare: 'The Peel Park *ace* stole in to add another to his season's tally'.

Trusty: Indicates a player's preferred foot and, as so often, used more of left than right: 'Fowler swung his *trusty* left boot and Howard *never saw* it'.

Tuck: 'Liam Lawrence, another close-season ***capture***, *cemented* Sunderland's third place with a second goal 13 minutes from time when he *tucked home* Michael Bridges' *lay-off*. The verb suggests a ***tidy*** finish, as well as in this case signalling that the game has been *put to bed*. These days when teams are often ***set up*** to play *narrow*, full backs or midfielders can be exhorted to *tuck in* so that the team keeps its ***shape***. The same pattern can be observed for the word *slot*, perhaps with more precision being suggested for a finish, and more tactical adjustment being implied for the change of formation: 'Gudjohnsen needed no second ***invitation*** to *slot home*'; 'Van Den Hauwe *slotted in* at centre half when we had injuries'.

Tumbling: How players are *sent* by over-robust ***tackles***. Strangely, nobody ever seems to be sent *tumbling* by fair ***challenges***; in these cases, they are more likely to be ***outmuscled***.

Turn round: 'Oh, they've not *turned us round*, have they?' The perils of drinking up late include scalding the roof of your mouth on a Pukka pie and suddenly realising, as your centre-forward *pops up* in your own box, that the away team has won the toss and changed ends, so denying you the opportunity to **suck** *the ball in* during the second half. *Turn round* can also work in a similar way to **kick-start**, especially if an improvement in form can be attributed to the efforts of one man: 'Darren's arrival has really *turned round* our season'; 'The new *gaffer* has *turned* things *round* here in a very short space of time'.

Turn up: 'We just didn't *turn up* first half and were lucky to go in one-down'. Manager-speak rather culti-vates the variations, as in these examples from Messrs Worthington, Slade and Holloway: 'We were still *on the coach* at three o'clock'; 'In the first half we weren't *at the races*'; 'In the second half we *stayed in the dressing room*'. Commentators fond of emphasising the inconsistency of a team will say 'it depends which Middlesbrough *turns up*'. Or this image may be rein-forced by a literary allusion – 'Our performances this year have been a bit *Jekyll and Hyde*' – a rather mundane adoption of the syndrome.

Turning point: All matches require (and all com-mentators seek) *a*, or better still *the*, *turning point*. They are conjectural and numerous at different points throughout a match – 'That *could prove* to be the *turn-ing point*' – before you settle on a single one at the end: 'The *turning point* in this one was without doubt Wouters' shoulder on Gascoigne'.

Two feet: 'He's got *two feet*'. What might seem a minimum requirement for a footballer is actually a considerable virtue, as players with *two feet* can use either effectively. For added emphasis say *two great* *feet*. Mind you, a *two-footed challenge* is not so clever, and these days usually merits a **straight** red.

Two minds: Not nearly as commendable as *two feet*. Defenders who get *caught in two minds* – for example, between a backpass or a clearance to *Row Z* – usually pay for it.

U

Ugly: Can qualify *tackle* or **incident**, but, with increasing frequency, it surfaces when a manager takes an almost perverse pleasure in **grinding out** results: 'This league's about hard work, *grafting*, sometimes playing *ugly*'. (Football managers are particularly known for preferring adjectives to adverbs, as in the now canonical *the **boys** done great*). Variants are being developed to describe pragmatic tactics which are certainly *not* **pretty**: 'Today we didn't play the *horrible* side of football very well'; 'Liverpool do not just *win ugly*, they border on the *grotesque*'. But the most imaginative development of the theme remains Ian Holloway's attempt to put a hard-fought victory at Chesterfield into 'gentleman's' terms: 'Our performance today would have been not the best looking bird, but at least we got her in the taxi'.

Unbeaten: Always combined with *run* (less often do you see 'losing runs', rather *losing sequences*). Alternatively to be used as a compliment, when teams *go* a certain number of games *unbeaten*.

Under: To *get it* or *bring it under* means to have successfully trapped an overhit pass or bobbling ball. *Control* is always understood.

Under the noses of: A phrase used when players are signed in a deal which may seem more scheming than *audacious*: 'Forlan was signed *under the noses of* Middlesbrough'.

Underdogs: Always *plucky* or *valiant* if they lose by less than three goals. Managers playing *mind-games* often aver that their team must *go down as*, or *be considered*, the *underdogs*.

Understudy: This noun spends most of its time in the realm of goalkeeping, where it is obvious that one particular player prevails at the expense of another: 'For so long the *understudy* to Grobbelaar, Bolder has decided to get *first-team football* at the Valley'. Other theatrical terms used in football include *curtain-raiser* (the *traditional* one in England being the Community, once the Charity, Shield), *cameo* and *performer* (as in 'useful *performer* on his day'). But when Freddie Shepperd *makes overtures* to a potential new manager he will not be humming the opening bars of *The Thieving Magpie*.

Undisclosed: A standard adjective when one of the parties to a transfer is too embarrassed to reveal the quantum of the fee, although often qualified by the phrase *thought to be in the region of* by journalists having a guess.

Unfancied: Adjective for teams that constitute a *surprise package*. *Unfancied* is not to be used in circumstances when it happens to be right not to fancy a team. You will rarely hear: '*Unfancied* Halifax duly lost by a *hatful*'.

Unfashionable: A polite way of saying 'unsuccess-ful', though the epithet can be used to highlight the current achievements of a club that is not traditionally in the running for *silverware*: 'Curbishley has worked wonders at *unfashionable* Charlton'.

Unforced error: Rare in football, certainly in comparison to other sports, but occasionally used of a misplaced clearance or backpass by tennis commentators earning a few bob over the winter at football matches.

Unleash: The most definitive verb for fierce shooting from longer range: 'Keith Gillespie *unleashed* a splendid volley from outside the area'. *Unfurl* can be used for crosses and free kicks but it overlaps to a considerable extent with *unleash*, as in the case of 'Hendrie *unfurling piledrivers* from distance'. We have found no example, though, of *unfurl* in company with the adjective *unstoppable*, which belongs instinctively with the more vigorous of the two verbs: 'Legg *unleashed* an *unstoppable* shot from 25 yards out'.

Unlock: Seems to have emerged almost as a technical term, even in countries where there is a different formation to undo than the *catenaccio*: 'More was required to *unlock* Middlesbrough's two *banks of four*'. Some managers may find that they have gone beyond worrying about the technicalities: 'Other teams don't *unlock* us. We *shoot ourselves in the foot*'.

Unnoticed: Strikers can *steal in*, especially at the *back stick*, *unnoticed*, but the word is also used to indicate the exploits of a club, usually provincial, who are not getting the *credit they deserve*: 'Norwich's charge up the table has gone largely *unnoticed* outside of Norfolk'.

Unsettled: Standard epithet for players who are likely to or have already put in a transfer request. Usually their stated grievance is a *lack of first-team football*.

Unveil: Your new *signing* will always be *unveiled* at a press conference. Perhaps the metaphor dates back to a time when the announcement of a new signing came as a surprise. Now that media coverage is so saturated, the veil is almost always translucent.

Unwanted: Can denote a player who is *out of favour* but more usually combined with *tag* or *nickname*: 'Southgate carries with him the *unwanted tag* of the man who missed the penalty'. When teams face some record-breaking ignominy – the first Premiership team to lose to non-league opposition, or the club to score fewest goals in a season – this *unwanted* achievement should be referred to as a *dubious honour*.

Up and down: 'Kieron Dyer gets *up and down* very well'. A locution referring not to a player's trampolining talents nor to prowess of any other sort, but to his ability to move swiftly from one end of the pitch to another, *box-to-box*. Such a player tends to have a good *engine*. In another sense, a good *up and down* does not in football refer to a neat chip and putt to escape with par, but a situation where a *dead-ball specialist* **shapes** the ball over the wall and under the bar.

Upend: 'Nicky Forster's dash into the box saw him *upended* by Gabor Gyepes'. While this verb could correctly describe what happens in many **no-nonsense** *challenges*, it tends to be used specifically of situations where an attacker has been **scythed** down in the penalty area, with the implication that the referee then *pointed to the spot*.

Utility player: A footballer whose versatility goes some way to compensate for a lack of ability. Or, perhaps more cruelly, a player supposedly good at everything but actually good at nothing. Often there is a faint hint that the player concerned does *anything asked* of him because he does not have the skill to *hold down* a **regular** position. Perhaps strengthened by usage in World War II when the word 'utility' stamped on consumer goods ensured no unnecessary extravagance. There may be brilliant *utility players*, **equally at home** in defence or mid-field (some of the Dutch **total footballers** come to mind) but they are spared this adjective which, as in 'utility room', describes something not only utilitarian but modest, perfunctory, to the point of being ignored.

V

Varsity Clash: Cambridge United v Oxford United. But their fans are about as likely to refer to the game in this way, as the students are to go to it. One of those terms, like **Battle of Britain**, wished upon football supporters by journalists.

Vintage: A slight upgrade on *trademark*. Add the player's first name for extra effect: 'That run and shot was absolutely *vintage* Michael Owen'. Or another way of putting it, from the restaurant rather than the wine cellar: 'That was a Michel Platini *special*'.

Virtual spectator: 'Preud'homme was a *virtual spectator* for the last twenty minutes'. This is how the goalkeeper on the dominant (usually winning) side should be described, the converse of the phrase **busier of the keepers**. Although such a bystander may

actually have done nothing but watch the game, the
virtual is necessary, lest you think the keeper went
and sat in one of the stands to do his watching.
It is incidentally unheard of to describe a football
supporter as a 'spectator'.

Vision: Rather like *awareness*, but this word pays
more extravagant tribute to the ability of the player
who has it. The noun does not always require an adjective (though players may be vouchsafed with *great
vision*). Nor should you specify of what the player
has *vision*. It is implicitly understood if you say 'Metgod
has *vision*' or 'Metgod's *vision* is brilliant' that this
is *vision* of team-mates whom he can bring into play
with a *defence-splitting* pass, and nothing to do with
his futuristic, utopian conceptualisations – or not necessarily: you never know with these intellectual foreign
players.

Visit: In an attempt to assign a gentlemanly quality
to a fixture, this noun is substituted for *clash* or
encounter. Used before and rarely after a game:
'County will be unchanged for the *visit* of Rovers'.
Similarly the plural noun *visitors* is used to denote the
opposition or away team, almost exclusively in polite
programme notes and on non-league scoreboards,
but occasionally also in press reports as a method of
avoiding repetition of the away team's name. Never
uttered by fans, be they the *home faithful* or the
travelling army.

W

Wage-bill: 'Despite a hefty increase on last year's
wage-bill, Arsenal's still looks miserly compared with

Manchester United's'. In football there does not seem to be such a thing as a 'payroll'; instead there is always a *wage-bill* which tends to *spiral out of control*.

Wake-up call: What superior teams may receive early in a game or season to ensure *complacency* does not *creep in*: 'The defeat at Chelsea was a real *wake-up call* and the **boys** have strung together some good results since then'. If it turns out the *wake-up call* is the presage of worse to come, then it will have been a *rude awakening*.

Walk: 'Leworthy really had to *walk* for that one'. Said of players who get their **marching orders** and can *have no complaints*. Perhaps it's because they will tend to trudge off the pitch more slowly than players being substituted. Or perhaps we are to understand that such players are *walking the plank*. At all events, it can be a *long* or *lonely walk* back to the dressing room. By contrast, if a team is having *a walk* or *a stroll in the park*, they are definitely in the **comfort zone**. A close cousin of **exhibition stuff**.

Waltz: 'McCarthy just *waltzed* past Drury there'. Perhaps because of their *dancing feet* or *twinkle toes*, this verb seems to be used primarily of wingers who are giving their full-backs a **torrid time**.

Want-away: Tabloid adjective for an **unsettled** player: '*Want-away* striker Frank Worthington *slapped in* another transfer request yesterday'. You never see: 'Frank Worthington, the striker who wants to leave Leicester'. A similar shorthand is in place for discontented supporters: 'The *stay-away* Dunfermline fans would be cursing their decision not to turn up as their team *stunned* the *visitors* with a first-half double'.

Warm the bench: 'Wycombe boss John Gorman insists he has not brought in on-loan goalkeeper Iain Turner just to *warm the bench* at the Causeway Stadium'. Managers and the *backroom staff* alongside them on the bench are never said to *warm* it. Substitutes alone are capable of this, apparently at the risk of spontaneous combustion: 'How can I keep Robbie Keane *on the bench* when he's *on fire*?'

Wasn't to know: The obligatory comment when a defender, especially a full-back with no attacker behind him, puts the ball out for a corner because he has not had a *shout*: 'A *needless* corner conceded by Burnley but McGreal did the right thing there – he *wasn't to know*'. The construction exonerates the defender more conclusively than would the words 'he didn't know'.

Watched: 'We've *had* Doncaster *watched* on several **occasions** and think we know a bit about them'. Although you can *run the rule over* a transfer target by having him *watched*, the word is more frequently used to describe *homework* on unfamiliar teams. These can be lower-division sides you have drawn in the cup or European opposition whose mysteries may require a *dossier* to be drawn up. But it is advisable to ensure that your *spies* have the right contact details: 'Geoff Taylor's *scouting report* to Ray Lewington backfired miserably as he accidentally faxed his observations to the wrong club, leaving the Lions squad reading with astonishment about their "cumbersome" defending. One was singled out as being an "*after you, Claude*" sort of player'.

Water carrier: A sobriquet particularly associated with Didier Deschamps, a typical *workhorse* who allowed others to *play* by doing the unglamorous jobs. Given the average length of his pass, he tried to make sure that he never had to *fetch and carry* very far. The phrase has become something of a compliment but was intended by Eric Cantona as an insult, especially as it alludes to one of the jobs of the *domestique* in cycling, who collects bidons of water from the team car and then pedals back to the peleton with them stuffed up his jersey so that his more senior team-mates can rehydrate without losing time on the road. Vinny Jones was a *hod carrier* in a previous life, and this term has been used for him and other midfielders not known for their creative skills.

Wave away: 'Appeals for a penalty were *waved away* by Martin Bodenham'. Describes the refusal of the referee to give a decision, even if he makes no hand signals at all, just as he can be said to *point to the spot* without actually pointing. The reported action has become such a proxy for a refusal to give a penalty decision that you do not even need to refer to appeals: 'Branch *tumbled* under a De Vos challenge and it looked a penalty – but referee Eddie Evans *waved it away*'.

Way: Rather pompously, a club can convince itself that it has a certain copyrighted style of play or code of ethics: 'Just *lumping* the ball upfield is not the Tottenham *way*'; 'Not pulling together for each other is just not the MK Dons *way*'. Coaching staff can congratulate themselves on methods purportedly unique to themselves: 'We've *certain ways* of *doing things* here at Hednesford Town **Football Club** and the players have to fit into that'. See also **all about**.

Wealth of experience: *Beleaguered* managers will announce a new **signing** in their programme notes with the phrase 'he brings with him a *wealth of experience* to the **football club**'. Such players are, of course, affordable veterans past their prime.

Wednesday night in Rochdale: The location is usually northern, the date invariably midweek for the emblematic, hypothetical fixture that a good player of suspect temperament (usually foreign) is unlikely to relish and will want to shirk. Often found in interrogative form: 'Passing it about on this stage is all very well, but can he do it on *a Tuesday night in Grimsby*?' The sobering rhetorical question is designed to check runaway enthusiasm for a superstar.

Week in week out: A phrase used to denote consistency, or the lack of it: 'Gough *performs* week in week out* and is a great example to the younger players'; 'We did well tonight but we have to string these performances together *week in week out*'. If surveying a whole career you can enlarge the scope to *year in year out*, and see *tracksuit manager* for an example of *day in day out* involvement. There is a related expression to chide a player for not doing something expected of him: 'Dublin should be winning the *aerial* challenges with Forssell *every day of the week*'.

Week's wages: The unit of measure for club fines, even if this usually gives no indication of the quantum of the penalty: 'Collymore was fined *two weeks' wages* for his latest indiscretion at La Manga'.

Weight: The *weight* or *burden of expectation* is what new managers or players at *a club as big as this* have to *deal with*. A *defence-splitting* pass is described as *well* or *perfectly weighted*. But, if the *wrong club* is used, passes are said to be *overhit*, not 'overweight'. A reluctance on the part of commentators to use this word of players is perhaps more understandable.

Welcome: As well as being a useful alternative to *versus* when reading out a cup draw on the radio – 'Barnsley *welcome* Plymouth Argyle' – the noun can appear euphemistically in managers' programme notes to incite booing of former *crowd favourites*: 'Hassan Kachloul was a *legend* here at Southampton and I'm sure you'll be giving him a *warm welcome* tonight'. We think Chris Coleman meant to refer to his **back four** more than elements in the Hammersmith End when promising Andy Cole a *welcoming committee* on his **return** to Craven Cottage. Similarly, commentators enjoy greeting a particularly *robust* tackle which leaves a *debutant* (usually a *fancy* foreign player) in the English game groaning, with the cheerfully ironic words: '*Welcome* to the **Premiership**, Juan Sebastian!'

Well documented: Euphemistic phrase to describe a matter that has been *all over the papers*. Often reserved for a managerial departure or the personal problems of a player: 'What happened at QPR has been *well documented*, and for the moment I'm concentrating on my media commitments'. Despite the documentation, the individual concerned, especially if he is Paul Merson, often then proceeds to talk about things again.

Well in: Many of the entries in this lexicon, whether they be well-worn clichés or delightfully inventive turns of phrase, were fashioned in the first place by the need for economy in live commentary and match reporting, most of which takes place to a tight deadline. The deadlines on the football pitch itself are even tighter, and what players shout there tends by necessity to be monosyllabic. These codewords and phrases are often repeated in the heat of battle by fans on the touchline or in the stands although, with exceptions like **anywhere** and **give and go**, not by commentators:

And again	I'm giving you the ball and I'm making a run on the presumption you'll give it me back (probably for the first time this season).
Back door	I'm behind you with better options – please back heel it to me at once.
Bring it	There's space in front of you, please push on into it to draw the defenders rather than waiting an age to pick your pass.
First one, ref	Even though that was a terrible challenge, it was my first such tackle in the game, so please do not caution me.
Get out	Not that it will make any difference but I'm willing that dangerous ball into our penalty area to roll out of play. (Can also be used as an alternative to *step up*).
Get rid	See *send it*.
Go home	Please pass it back to the keeper instead of taking any risks in this situation.
Gone, ref	That ball which the opposition touched last has indisputably left the field of play.
Have it	Yes, it was a village clearance into somebody's back garden but we've all seen that Peter Kay commercial.
Jack's	I'm not allowed to say 'leave it' because that's against the rules, but you all know that's what I mean, and we might even get Jamie Cureton sent off.

Man on	Sorry, I've just played you a hospital pass and a member of the opposition is about to go straight through you, so be aware.
Name on it	To avoid further confusion, would somebody in our defence please nominate themselves immediately to head this ball into our box away from danger?
One each	Can we all please pick up the man we've been detailed to mark at this set piece rather than ball watching?
One more	There's a man on the overlap unmarked, please either step over the ball or help it on to him without further delay or dallying on the ball.
One of you	Rather than colliding into each other in comical fashion and presenting the opposition with a chance on a plate, please decide which of you should deal with this situation.
Options	It's our throw-in/free-kick, can somebody actually make a run into space so that the man taking it has someone to hit?
Our ball, ref	It probably isn't ours but you expect both sides to stick their hands up whenever the ball goes out of play, so I won't disappoint you.
Send it	Never mind about dribbling it out of defence like a Brazilian, please bang it upfield immediately as there's still a potentially dangerous situation here in our box.

Skills   Allow me to purr with pleasure at
                    the piece of business you've just
                    pulled off, particularly as it might
                    wind up the opposition further.

Step up   Can we all please push upfield in uni-
                    son right now because if we all just
                    stand here too deep after clearing
                    this one there'll be another ball to
                    deal with in a second?

Time   Even a player of your moderate
                    ability has the time and space here
                    to look up and decide at reasonable
                    leisure which is the best option.

Time, ref   I humbly submit that the opposition
                    are cynically running down the
                    clock, please stop your watch and
                    book one of them.

To feet   How many times do I have to ask you
                    not to hoof it hopefully in the air
                    when I'm five foot eight and my
                    marker is six foot four?

Well in   That really was an exceptionally
                    good tackle, and as a bonus we might
                    have even taken a bit of man as well
                    as ball.

Well watched: *Well watched* is the expression if a
goalkeeper or defender *deals with* a cross into the
mix by not actually playing the ball. Almost a reflex
in these circumstances, but sometimes used with
heavy irony: 'Let's just say that was *well watched* by
Geoff Crudgington'.

Wembley: There was a time when the world knew
only two *twin towers*. Now there are four and yet

none. *The Empire Stadium,* like the World Trade
Center, is no longer. Comparisons end there. *Wembley*
had always been a destination more imagined and
hoped for than it was experienced and arrived at
by most fans (hence *the road to Wembley* and *Wembley
way,* set phrases which added to the mystique of
the FA Cup as a sort of Holy Grail). Yet there was
a void in the language of football during the period
in which the *new Wembley* was being built. The
special ***energy-sapping*** properties of its turf cannot
be found in Cardiff or at any other grounds. While
Wembley was there, it seemed easier to believe that
a supernatural force, against the odds and beyond
rational comprehension, was impelling you because
your *name was on the Cup.* While the stadium
was being redeveloped, the fatalistic cup song – '*Que
Serà Serà,* whatever will be will be' – languished without a rhyme. Now these ***traditions*** will be restored,
along with the new ground in all its ***Corinthian***
splendour.

Wheel away: The action of a scorer in the immediate
aftermath of scoring. At such moments the *wheeling
away* is performed in *celebration, delight* or *triumph.*
Very commonly seen in the captions to photographs
in programmes or newspapers, taken just after
the ball has hit the ***back of the net.*** Not to be confused with *reel away,* which players sometimes do, in
theatrical fashion, if there has been the *suspicion* of
a headbutt.

Wheeling and dealing: What ***cash-strapped*** managers are always required to do: 'At Millwall, Benny
Fenton's reputation for *wheeling and dealing* preceded
him'. The analogy with the used-car trade is not too
far away: 'Berger was the archetypal Harry Redknapp
transfer – a player with a *sublime* left foot and a few
miles on the clock'.

Whip: Balls, especially crosses, hit with pace and a spiteful degree of *curl* are said to have *whip* on them. The Big-Ronism was *big ugly whip*. There are alternatives for the *action* a player puts on a dead ball: 'Teddy said he put so much *gear* on the free kick that it swerved at the last moment'.

Whistler: Thesaurus-driven alternative to *referee*: 'The Melton Mowbray *whistler* was **spot on** five minutes later'. *Arbiter* is another option encouraged by a similar desire not to repeat yourself.

White line: 'We respect France but once we step over *that white line* in Portugal all that will go *out of the window*'; 'He's a lovely **lad** but sometimes, when he gets over *that white line* on a Saturday afternoon, the red mist descends'. Football people specifically call to mind the markings on the perimeter of the pitch when they want to emphasise that they are crossing a threshold.

Width: A footballing elixir, possessed by all effective *attacking units*. Teams that *lack width* really ought to go out and buy a *winger* or two. But *width* does not just mean **wingers**. The abstraction seems to be used all the more since the advent of *wing-backs* in the modern game, who *augment* the attack by *providing width*.

Will: Peter Jones, the lamented radio commentator of the 1970s and 1980s, liked a future tense when describing a match in real time: 'Case *will **find*** Heighway, who *will* pass back to Callaghan, who *will* ...'. Perhaps this mannerism served to disguise the fact that, like all radio commentators, he was always a little behind play, or perhaps it lent to the passing moves he so evocatively described an aura of synergetic inevitability.

Wily: Often combined with *old campaigner* or *fox*. Can be used of a ***midfield general*** or an experienced centre-half (particularly if he is South American and playing in Italy), but also of managers famed for their tactical acumen, their motivational powers or for their ***wheeling and dealing***.

Win: The noun is interchangeable with *victory*, except faintly nationalistic hues may surface in the latter case: 'England are now *in the driving-seat* in group D, after their *heroic victory* over Turkey'. A *win* at club level is less likely to be glorious, as in the truism that *a win is a win*, and managers celebrate *coming away* or *getting away* with a *win* of any kind, even if it is ***ugly***. In radio commentaries the verb is used much less obtrusively to indicate the capture of possession, particularly in ***aerial battles***: 'Phil Chapple has *won* so much in the air tonight'. Whereas a *ballwinner* tends to *win* the ball on the ***deck***.

Winger: Even though they are supposed to provide ***width***, *wingers* seem to be criticised more often than players in other positions for being ***peripheral***. Perhaps this is because they are considered easier to ***kick*** or *mark out of the game*, or because a certain breed of *mercurial winger* can be a *luxury* item. Ever since Alf Ramsey's *wingless wonders*, it seems, the more industrious *wide man* has been on the verge of superseding the *old-fashioned winger*. Sometimes factors other than ***work-rate*** and the ability to *run at* defenders are brought to bear in deciding upon the correct title: 'There has been some discussion as to whether Tottenham's *chunky* Andy Reid is a *proper winger* or a *wide player*'.

Winner: The decisive or deciding goal. Football reporters tend to be careful, perhaps a bit ponderous, in indicating that you do not know that a goal is a *winner* until the end of the match. Thus: 'On 35 minutes, Iwelumo hit what turned out to be the *winner*'. The verbs to *turn out* or to *prove* ensure retrospective precision in these cases.

Withdraw: Strikers may be described as *withdrawn* or playing in a *withdrawn role*. This denotes the act of dropping *deep* rather than introspection of any kind. When managers *withdraw a player* to make a substitution (rather than *removing* the player or *taking him off* the pitch) this more temperate verb may help to give the impression that the manager is thinking *tactically*.

Wives and girlfriends: Progressive managers will allow the players away on international *duty* a day or two with *wives and girlfriends*. The language of football has not got round to calling them anything else, maybe because *partners* is a term which is already taken.

Wobble: A *wobble* (*wobbler* if you are Andy Townsend) occurs at moments when a team likely to win the league suffers an unexpected setback: 'Arsenal had a little *wobble* at the Reebok, but still should be good enough to clinch the title'. Two Liverpool keepers are now celebrated for their goal-line *wobbles,* otherwise known as *spaghetti-legs,* in European finals.

Wonderkid: Or *boy wonder*. An exceptional *product* of a team's *youth policy*. Sometimes translated back into its German antecedent, as in 'Leeds's *Wunderkind*, Aaron Lennon'.

Woodwork: The accepted noun for the description of post and/or crossbar, even though the frames of the goal are no longer wooden: 'It was just not Darlington's day. The Quakers hit the *woodwork* yet again ten minutes from time.' Less specific but also less ambiguous than saying 'the Quakers hit the bar again'.

Words: *Harsh* or *choice* ones can be *said* or *had* at half-time; *heated* ones in the tunnel (whereas the euphemistic ***pleasantries*** tend to be exchanged on the pitch or in front of the ***dugouts***). Strangely, referees *have a word*, usually a *quiet* one, rather than *words*. *Talks* are more reserved for transfer negotiations: they are *opened* with a player, often *stall* or are *put on hold*, and then are *completed* or *called off*.

Work the keeper: The work ethic can come to the fore when a summariser is commenting on a disappointing finish – 'He should at least have *made* Jim Platt *work* from there' – or exhorts a side in a more partisan way to *get more shots in* on goal: 'They did well enough but really need to *work the keeper over* in the second half'.

Work-rate: A comparatively recent term, its pseudo-scientific flavour suited to a generation weaned on Carling Opta statistics and Fantasy Football points. It really means *effort* and *application* but perhaps something more too, like a willingness to chase ***lost causes*** (as in 'Savage's *work-rate* was phenomenal') which, in football, is a virtue: 'We've got to match them for *work-rate*, if we're going to get anything out of the game'. See also ***industry***.

Worry about that: 'De Vries' shot took a *wicked deflection* on its way in, but Leicester *won't worry about that*'; 'Drogba ***scuffed*** that one really, but *he won't worry about that*'. This verbal tic of commentary (after a lucky goal) comes close to admitting its own redundancy. Good strikers are only ever seen ***queueing up*** in the six yard box, never for stress and anxiety counselling.

Wraps: What new signings or, more occasionally, new tactics, are *kept under*. Similar ideas are treating a youngster with *kid gloves* and wrapping your more fragile stars in *cotton wool*.

Wrecking ball: 'Stuart Elliot *latched on* to Danny Allsopp's knock down and *blasted* past Jones with that *wrecking ball* of a left foot'; 'Robben's *twinkle-toed* dexterity *set up* Lampard 25 yards out, his *wrecking ball* of a right foot sending a rising drive past Green's *flailing* right hand'. An image for the shooting foot of a player renowned for his *strikes* from distance so graphic as to be surreal, especially as it is of one ball hitting another. Perhaps developed from the journalistic formula of a boxer's *wrecking ball* right hook. Teams on the receiving end are sometimes duly *demolished*, although such heavy plant and machinery is not recommended for close control: 'Djibril Cissé came on to demonstrate the deft touch of a *wrecking ball*'.

Wrong club: 'Solano looked up and saw Hendrie in *acres* of *space* on the right but hit his crossfield pass with the *wrong club* into the stand'. Golf is a favourite recreational activity of footballers and a few of its terms enter the lexicon, such as this colourful expression to indicate a misjudgement of distance. Players can also *tee up* a shot for a team-mate who might then *snaphook* it wide. Meanwhile, goalkeepers with *dodgy distribution* can be criticised for the *persistent fade* on their kicks. Compare also *miskick* and *tap-in*.

X

X-rated: Censorious certification of tackles which are *over the top* in every sense, or of games where there have been many such tackles: 'Simon Charlton was furious with Jody Morris after his *x-rated lunge*'; 'Once referee Riley lost his grip on proceedings, the game descended into *real x-rated stuff*'. In some of these *horror shows*, it is the incompetence rather than the violence of the defending that might cause the manager to hide in the *dugout* or the long-suffering *faithful* to cover their eyes: 'For Norwich fans and any *neutral* observer, the 4–4 draw was compulsive viewing but for all Boro supporters the finale was *x-rated material'*. There are no other gradations of rating, like PG or 18, in football parlance.

Y

Yard: Standard imperial unit of measure for *pace*. Some players are unfortunate to *lack* a *yard of pace* to begin with, others *lose* it as they get older. In the plural, used to indicate how far a forward has strayed past the *last man*, especially in *situations* where the linesman does not raise his flag and said player is *controversially ruled onside*: 'Butragueño looked *yards off* there but was allowed to go on'. *A mile* is the alternative to *yards* in this context.

Ye: The archaic second-person form can yet be heard on two occasions in Britain. On Sundays: '*Ye* Holy Angels Bright'; on Saturdays: 'Come on *ye* Blu-ues'. *You* can now be used in its stead, in both cases.

Your: '*Your* Klinsmanns, *your* Stoichkovs…'. The second-person possessive allied to a plural guarantees the sententious force of this phrase. The plural has the paradoxical effect of pointing up the uniqueness of the player: 'To compete with *your* Zidanes, *your* Henrys, you have to be a bit special'. See also *the likes of*.

Youth policy: Always seems to be *progressive* or *forward-looking*, and bears fruit in the shape of *products* *of the youth scheme* or *youth products*. When it works superlatively well, you may talk of a *production line of talent*. The League Cup now exists chiefly to give the managers of big clubs a chance to *blood* youngsters.

Yo-yo: 'Birmingham City's somewhat dubious distinction at the turn of the century lay in trying their best to equal Darwen's anti-evolutionary record of *up-down-up-down*'. This historian of the Football League was writing before it became fashionable to refer to the *yo-yo effect* when accounting for the movement of a club between two divisions, too good for one and too poor for the other. Sheffield Wednesday were the *yo-yo team* of the 1950s, probably in the heyday of the *yo-yo*, which has fended off more modern counterparts to describe the recent exploits of *your* Leicesters and *your* Sunderlands. A connected joke is the description of Walsall as champions of the old Division Four or Lecce as champions of Serie B *every other year*.

Z

Z: *Row Z* is a long way from the pitch and so, by inference, the hypothetical destination of any **no-nonsense** clearance. Defenders who put *safety first* by playing *within their limitations* can be praised, but a reference to the back of the stand may also depict a badly over-hit pass: 'He tried to find Fredgaard on the other wing, but that's gone straight into *Row Z*'. Old-school managers may even condone their players putting the opposition into the crowd along with the ball: 'County boss Billy Dearden was left *fuming*: "O'Driscoll should have finished in *Row Z* but we were too nice"'.

Acknowledgements

Leigh and Woodhouse would like to thank the readers, listed below with their club allegiances where known, who made suggestions for the paperback edition:

Phil Adey (Wolverhampton Wanderers), Paul Akelele (Bradford City), Jeremy Ainsley (San Jose Earthquakes), Ray Berger (Arsenal), James Bewley (Southampton), Rob Bishop (Aston Villa), John Blain, James Bowers (Huddersfield Town), Garry Bushell (West Ham United), Gus Campbell (Crystal Palace), David Cardwell (Derby County), Michael Carey, Charles Catchpole (Norwich City), Adrian Chiles (West Bromwich Albion), Ian Colley (Sheffield Wednesday), James Cox (Hereford United), Paul Coyte (Tottenham Hotspur), Mark Devery, Nick Dowell (Liverpool), Michael Drake (Norwich City), Martin Eales (Bristol City), Bill Eaton, Frank Edwards (Barnet), Sean Fitzgerald (Chelsea), Jake Fowler (Everton), Tom Freestone, Neil Fung-on (Crystal Palace), Neil Gibbs (Manchester United), Roy Gibson (Manchester City), Steve Goodman (unattached), Dave Green (Blackburn Rovers),

Martin Gunning, Rich Guy (Aston Villa), Nick Hammond (Sunderland), James Hanning (Chelsea), John Harris, David Hart, Glyn Heighway, David Herbert (Everton), Sam Hayward (Southampton), Dan Higgins (Charlton Athletic), Clive Holes (Wolverhampton Wanderers), Tim Hopkins (Hertfordshire Schools), Nick Hunter (Nottingham Forest), Hugh Johnstone (Aston Villa), Andrew Jones, Danny Kelly (Tottenham Hotspur), Neil Kenny (Kingstonian), Richard Kershaw (Liverpool), Robert Langham (Reading), Ian Leigh (Sheffield Wednesday), Michael Leigh (Reading), Ron Leigh (Sheffield Wednesday), Karl Leydecker (Liverpool/ Kaiserslautern), Graeme Liveston (Dundee United), James Lloyd (Aston Villa), Chris Lowe, Josh Lury (Arsenal), Justin Maude (Liverpool), Bernard McGinley, Gavin McGrath (Huddersfield Town), John Mehaffey (Reuters), Earl O'Keeffe (Queen's Park Rangers), George Pagliero (Old Robsonians), Ian Perks, Mariya Petkova (CSKA Sofia), Martyn Pilley (Middlesbrough), Jonathan Pritchard (Aston Villa), Jamie Reeves (Southend United), Will Rhode (Aston Villa), Neill Ross (Tottenham Hotspur), Kiaran Saunders (Sheffield United), Mike Scofield (Watford), Nigel Shardlow (Derby County), Rob Smith (Aston Villa), Peter Straus (Chelsea), Rob Sutton (West Ham United), Ian Tatley (Wigan Athletic), Greg Thomas (Liverpool), Ian Thrupp (Aston Villa), Jon Tipple (Queen's Park Rangers), Katharina Tozer (Sheffield Wednesday), Robin van Koert (FC Den Bosch), Alex Viac (Liverpool), Nick White (West Ham United), Camilla Wilks (Arsenal), Keith Wilks (Dundee), Frank Woodhouse (West Bromwich Albion), Jonty Woodhouse (Aston Villa), Melba Woodhouse (Aston Villa), Peter Woodward, Paul Woolfson (Sheffield Wednesday), Jim Wynn (Leeds United)